ITIL® 4 Direct, Plan and Improve (DPI)

Your companion to the ITIL 4 Managing Professional and Strategic Leader DPI certification

ITIL® 4 Direct, Plan and Improve (DPI)

Your companion to the ITIL 4 Managing Professional and Strategic Leader DPI certification

CLAIRE AGUTTER

itgp™

IT Governance Publishing

Every possible effort has been made to ensure that the information contained in this book is accurate at the time of going to press, and the publisher and the author cannot accept responsibility for any errors or omissions, however caused. Any opinions expressed in this book are those of the author, not the publisher. Websites identified are for reference only, not endorsement, and any website visits are at the reader's own risk. No responsibility for loss or damage occasioned to any person acting, or refraining from action, as a result of the material in this publication can be accepted by the publisher or the author.

ITIL® is a registered trademark of AXELOS Limited. All rights reserved.

Apart from any fair dealing for the purposes of research or private study, or criticism or review, as permitted under the Copyright, Designs and Patents Act 1988, this publication may only be reproduced, stored or transmitted, in any form, or by any means, with the prior permission in writing of the publisher or, in the case of reprographic reproduction, in accordance with the terms of licences issued by the Copyright Licensing Agency. Enquiries concerning reproduction outside those terms should be sent to the publisher at the following address:

IT Governance Publishing Ltd
Unit 3, Clive Court
Bartholomew's Walk
Cambridgeshire Business Park
Ely, Cambridgeshire
CB7 4EA
United Kingdom
www.itgovernancepublishing.co.uk

© Claire Agutter 2021

The author has asserted the rights of the author under the Copyright, Designs and Patents Act, 1988, to be identified as the author of this work.

First edition published in the United Kingdom in 2021 by IT Governance Publishing

ISBN 978-1-78778-282-2

FOREWORD

Congratulations on purchasing *ITIL® 4 Direct, Plan and Improve (DPI) – Your companion to the ITIL 4 Managing Professional and Strategic Leader DPI certification*. In my opinion, the title perfectly describes the real value and purpose of the book. It is an invaluable source of guidance when preparing for the Direct, Plan and Improve certification, but perhaps more importantly, it serves as a critical companion for all professionals tasked with "setting strategy".

Having read numerous service management guides and strategy books over the years, this one stands apart from the others as it combines the necessary revision support with a more practical and real-world focus. Throughout the book, the author's guidance is mirrored by my own experience in defining, implementing, and driving an improved service management strategy in numerous organisations. For example, whilst the book quite rightly references the significance of digital transformation and the impact it has on an organisation, it is the guidance around maintaining a pragmatic and flexible approach that is key. This is reinforced by the author highlighting the significance of ensuring strategic considerations remain flexible where possible and that cultural inertia e.g. the human factor, varied communication etc. are included in the planning process.

As a revision guide, this book does an excellent job of summarising all the key points and information into one area and provides valuable context to complex and challenging subjects. This combined with the signposting of future reading and additional sources of information, make the

Foreword

book an essential companion in preparing for the exam, and afterward, as you apply these new skills on your career journey.

Rob Ford
Senior ITSM consultant

ABOUT THE AUTHOR

Claire Agutter is a service management trainer, consultant and author. In 2020, she was one of Computer Weekly's Top 50 Most Influential Women in Tech. In 2018 and 2019 she was recognised as an HDI Top 25 Thought Leader and was part of the team that won itSMF UK's 2017 Thought Leadership Award. Claire provides regular, free content to the IT service management (ITSM) community as the host of the popular ITSM Crowd hangouts, and is the chief architect for VeriSM™, the service management approach for the digital age. Claire is the director of ITSM Zone, which provides online IT service management training, and Scopism, a content and consulting organisation and the publisher of the SIAM Body of Knowledge.

After providing support to thousands of people taking ITIL training and certification from version 2 onwards, she has created this series of books for those studying towards ITIL 4 Managing Professional and Strategic Leader status.

For more information, please see:

- *https://itsm.zone*
- *www.scopism.com*

Contact: *www.linkedin.com/in/claireagutter/*.

ACKNOWLEDGEMENTS

I would like to thank Dr. Suzanne Van Hove for her support with reviewing the practical sections, and for providing advice while I was writing the book.

CONTENTS

Introduction 1
   How to use this book 1
Chapter 1: Direct, plan and improve key concepts 5
   Direction 5
   Planning 6
   Improvement 8
   Operating model 9
   Methods 10
   Risks 10
   Controls 10
   Scope of control 11
   Vision and mission 13
   Strategy, tactics and operations 14
   Governance, compliance and management 16
   Policies, controls and guidelines 19
   Value, outcomes, costs and risks 21
Chapter 2: DPI scope, key principles and methods 23
   Cascading objectives 23
   Cascading requirements 25
   Decision-making 26
   Defining effective policies, controls and guidelines 28
Chapter 3: The role of governance, risk and compliance 31
   Risks and controls 31
   Risk and direction 32
   Risk and improvement 37
   DPI and governance 37
   Governance structures 38
   Governance of the service provider 39
   Placing decision-making at the right level 40

Ensuring controls are sufficient but not excessive 40
Chapter 4: Focus on improvement 43
Creating a continual improvement culture 43
Continual improvement of the service value chain and practices 45
Continual improvement in organisations 46
The continual improvement model 47
Assessments 57
Building a business case 77
Improvement reviews 81
Analysis of lessons learned 82
Embedding an improvement culture 85
Chapter 5: Focus on organisational change management 87
The nature of OCM 87
OCM and DPI 91
The purpose of OCM 93
OCM key terms and concepts 94
Emotional, social and system intelligence 96
Values-based organisational change 98
Organisational change principles 100
The scope of OCM 102
OCM practice success factors 107
Key metrics 111
OCM and communication 114
Stakeholder identification and management 114
Stakeholder communication 117
Communication is a two-way process 119
The message is the medium 121
Communication methods and media 121
Defining and establishing feedback channels 124
OCM throughout the service value chain 125
Interfaces across the value chain 125

Contents

Chapter 6: DPI, measurement and reporting 129
   Measurement and reporting basics 130
   Reasons for measuring 132
   Types of measurements 135
   Measurement and behaviour 138
   Measurement cascades and hierarchies 138
   Success factors and KPIs 147
   SMART 148

Chapter 7: DPI, value streams and practices 151
   Value streams and processes in the Service Value
   System 151
   Value streams and practices 153
   Value streams and processes 155
   Measurement and the four dimensions 156
   Ensuring and using feedback 163
   Value stream mapping 164
   Workflow optimisation 170
   Considerations for efficient design 171
   Theory of constraints 173
   Kanban 174

Chapter 8: Exam preparation 177

Appendix: Banksbest case study 181
   Company overview 181
   Company structure 182
   Future plans 183
   IT services 183
   IT department 184
   IT service management 185
   Sample employee biographies 185

Further reading 187

INTRODUCTION

How to use this book

The majority of this book is based on the *ITIL® 4 Strategist – Direct, Plan & Improve (DPI)* publication and the associated DPI Strategist syllabus. DPI is the only one of the ITIL 4 advanced level courses that contributes to both Managing Professional (MP) and Strategic Leader (SL) status.

In addition to helping you prepare for your certification, I also want to give you some advice and guidance that will lead to you using this book once your training and exam are over. I've added some of my own practical experience to this book and given you advice and some points to think about along the way. My goal is for you to refer back to this book in years to come, not just put it away once you've passed your exam. With this additional content, you'll find this book is an excellent supplement to any training course and a useful tool in your ongoing career.

As you read the book, assume that all the content is related to the syllabus unless it is highlighted in one of two ways:

Introduction

Something for you: a small exercise for you to complete to apply the ITIL 4 concepts in your own role, or a point for you to think about. This content is not examinable.

Practical experiences: any content marked with this image is based on my own experiences and is not examinable.

The content highlighted as something for you or practical experiences might also refer to the Banksbest case study you can find in the Appendix. I'll use the case study to give an example of how something would work in the real world, or to help you apply what you're reading about. Case studies can really help to bring abstract concepts to life. The case study is not examinable but using it will help you get a deeper understanding of the DPI concepts you are learning. Let's start with something for you now:

Introduction

> **?**
>
> Why not read the case study and make a note of your first impressions of the Banksbest organisation and its plans before you study the DPI content in this book?

Unless stated otherwise, all quotations are from *ITIL® 4 Direct, Plan and Improve* and *Practice Guides* published by AXELOS in 2020. Copyright © AXELOS Limited 2020. Used under permission of AXELOS Limited. All rights reserved.

CHAPTER 1: DIRECT, PLAN AND IMPROVE KEY CONCEPTS

This chapter introduces the DPI key concepts that underpin the rest of the DPI content. These include:

- DPI key terms;
- Differentiating between key concepts, including:
  - Vision and mission;
  - Strategy, tactics, operations;
  - Governance, compliance, management; and
  - Policies, controls, guidelines.
- Value, outcomes, costs and risks in a DPI context.

The ITIL 4 DPI manual is intended to support practitioners at all levels:

"Regardless of organizational role, everyone has authority, even if it is limited to personal direction. Everyone should plan. And everyone should be contributing to, if not leading, improvement. The publication explores and explains principles, methods, and techniques that can be universally used to direct, plan, and improve. We have also included tools and templates that can be used to implement the guidance."

The key themes within DPI are the focus of the DPI course, and of this publication.

Direction

The definition of direction is:

1: Direct, plan and improve key concepts

"Leading, conducting, or guiding someone, or ordering something. This includes setting and communicating the vision, purpose, objectives, and guiding principles for an organization or team. It may also include leading or guiding the organization or team towards its objectives."

Having clear direction in an organisation helps to clarify what outcomes are expected and what principles should be followed. Effective direction relies on a defined mission, respect for the abilities of those being directed, and good two-way communication. Changes in direction need to be communicated so that team members can adapt to them.

The people who give direction may have been given authority formally (for example, they hold a senior role such as a chief technology officer) or informally (for example, an enthusiastic champion for a new initiative). **Evaluate, direct and monitor** (EDM) is a common construct for providing direction. EDM allows performance to be monitored to ensure direction is having some effect.

Planning

Planning is defined in ITIL 4 as the *"value chain activity that ensures a shared understanding of the vision, current status, and improvement direction for all four dimensions and all products and services across an organization"*.

Once direction is set and provides an objective, a plan can be used to define how to move towards the desired state. Plans help to avoid waste and reduce risk and are particularly important in large organisations where more coordination is needed.

1: Direct, plan and improve key concepts

Plans can range from very simple to very complicated. Planning too much or too little creates problems; for example:

- Too much planning means actual execution can be delayed;
- Too much faith in detailed plans leads to paralysis when something unexpected happens; and
- Work starts without sufficient planning, leading to rework or waste.

The amount of planning undertaken should be proportionate to the work that is being carried out. Planning is helpful, but it's important to remember that plans may need to evolve once work begins or as requirements change. Planning should be seen as an iterative activity that continues alongside the work being carried out, rather than a one-off exercise.

"Everyone has a plan until they get punched in the mouth" (Mike Tyson).

In the year that I wrote this book, a pandemic crippled economies around the world and changed every aspect of daily life. Planning is a vital capability, but we must also build resilient organisations that can adapt and change when circumstances deviate from the plan.

1: Direct, plan and improve key concepts

Improvement

Improvement is defined as *"a deliberately introduced change that results in increased value for one or more stakeholders"*.

Very few organisations start with a completely blank canvas. If we are dealing with existing people, processes or technology, our activities are improvement activities. To measure whether an improvement has been effective, we must understand our start point and whether the change has made things 'better'. Improvement can apply to any part of the ITIL service value system.

Improvement takes place at every level of an organisation – strategic, tactical and operational. If operational staff are empowered to identify and (where appropriate) implement improvements, organisations can see real gains in their services and the user experience that they offer. Different levels of the organisation might have a different role to play in improvement, with direction set at the strategic level, planning and coordination taking place at the tactical level, and implementation taking place at the operational level. It is important to remember that the staff who are closest to the customer may be best placed to identify improvements.

Measurement and reporting help us understand our position before, during and after improvement activities. Objective data means there should be no argument about whether something is 'better' or not. Measurement and reporting can also help predict the results of improvement actions, for example how many more website sales would be generated with an improved checkout process?

1: Direct, plan and improve key concepts

> One of the advantages of starting something in a 'greenfield environment' (i.e. one where nothing is already in place) is the complete freedom from constraints and past experience. When we approach improvement activities, we need to build a plan that incorporates past experiences, culture, existing technology, and so on. This can create challenges that need to be part of our improvement plans. For example, in the case study in the Appendix you read about the rebrand from HW Banking to Banksbest. If Banksbest were launched as a brand-new organisation, it would be easier for it to communicate its 'digital first' message. Because Banksbest is an 'improved' brand compared to HW Banking, it must consider the existing customer base and their perception of the old and new brands.

Operating model

An operating model is *"a conceptual and/or visual representation of how an organization co-creates value with its customers and other stakeholders, as well as how the organization runs itself"*.

The ITIL service value chain is an operating model for the creation, delivery and management of products and services. Operating models show complex systems divided into sub-systems, allowing them to be examined and managed more easily.

1: Direct, plan and improve key concepts

Methods

A method is *"a way, technique, or process for doing something. Methods are structured and systematic."*

Methods are used for structured, systematic work. Some organisations provide guidance about which methods to use, and others allow teams carrying out work to choose their own method. For example, some organisations will work in a waterfall way, whereas others use Agile methods. Waterfall or Agile could be mandatory for teams, or teams might be allowed to choose their own ways of working.

Risks

Risk is *"a possible event that could cause harm or loss or make it more difficult to achieve objectives. Risk can also be defined as uncertainty of outcome and can be used in the context of measuring the probability of positive outcomes as well as negative outcomes."*

Every organisation will experience risk. From a DPI perspective, risk management is a way of balancing maximum results against minimum harm or loss. Once risks are understood, they need to be managed. Risk management is important because risks can cause projects, products and services to fail or deliver sub-standard results. If team members are aware of risks that are being ignored, this can affect their behaviour and morale. Ultimately, organisations need to understand their current risk levels to drive improvement activities. Risks cannot be managed until they are understood.

Controls

A control is *"the means of managing a risk, ensuring that a business objective is achieved, or that a process is followed"*.

1: Direct, plan and improve key concepts

Controls are used as safeguards or countermeasures. Control categories include:

- **Organisational/procedural controls:** These controls include policies, organisation, training, ownership and processes.
- **Logical/technical controls:** These include elements like required fields, scripting and automated workflows.
- **Physical controls:** These include badge or code entry systems, fencing, locks and guards.

Controls need to be measured to assess their effectiveness. They form part of 'direction' from a DPI perspective as they can be used to enforce directives.

Scope of control

Scope of control is a term that defines the *"area(s) or activities over which a person has the authority to direct the actions of others or define the required outcomes"*.

The ITIL 4 DPI guidance is relevant for anyone at any level of an organisation but needs to be understood through the lens of their own 'scope of control'. An individual's scope of control might only include themselves and their own activities, or it might incorporate a whole organisation. The scope of control is different to someone's 'scope of influence', which can allow them to create change in areas where they don't have formal control. Influencing and cooperation can be more effective than formal direction.

1: Direct, plan and improve key concepts

One UK government organisation that I worked with outsourced its IT operations to an external service provider. During the outsourcing exercise, trade union representatives fought to minimise the number of tasks and the level of responsibility that was transferred away from the government staff currently in post. Poor transition management led to a situation where the external service provider was contractually required to deliver agreed IT outcomes but was hindered in its role by the government department's own staff. If the external service provider missed one of its targets, it would usually avoid any penalties due to mitigating circumstances related to the actions of government staff. The scope of control had been defined for an ideal world, which then led to problems when it was implemented in the real world. The external service provider was in the difficult position of trying to deliver outcomes in an ecosystem it did not have control over. The government staff experienced low morale and a lack of clarity about their own roles and responsibilities.

Over time, the 'scope of influence' became much more important to successful service provision for this contract. Better working relationships developed between the external service provider's staff and the government staff. Informal agreements were reached, and work began to happen much more smoothly.

1: Direct, plan and improve key concepts

Vision and mission

You need to understand the definitions of vision and mission, as well as the differences between them.

A vision is a *"defined aspiration of what an organization would like to become in the future"*. Visions are used to show employees what the future could look like. This helps them buy into the vision, maintain their motivation and understand why certain actions are taken.

A mission is a *"short but complete description of the overall purpose and intentions of an organization"*.

Many organisations have formal 'mission statements' that are published inside and outside the organisation. Teams will work towards the mission, so it is good practice to define initiatives and activities that will help them do this.

Do you know the vision of the organisation you work for, or the one you have worked for most recently? Can you think of any famous examples of visions that inspired you? How about this, from 1980?

"A computer on every desk and in every home."

– Bill Gates, Microsoft® chairman and chief executive officer, 1980

1: Direct, plan and improve key concepts

Strategy, tactics and operations

Organisations will usually plan at different levels: strategic, tactical and operational. Lower-level plans normally include greater detail. All levels of plans should be aligned and linked to the overall organisational objectives.

An organisation's **strategy** will help it achieve its objectives. The strategy should then cascade down to lower-level strategies for departments, locations or other organisational elements.

A strategy is *"a broad approach or course of action defined by an organization for achieving its objectives"*.

Take a look at the Banksbest case study in the Appendix if you haven't done so already. Banksbest has defined three strategic goals:

- To be the tenth largest provider of business banking services in the UK (growing its customer base by approximately 25%).
- To grow its residential mortgage business by 50%.
- To build a reputation as a 'digital first' banking provider.

Two of these goals will be relatively simple to measure, based on the growth of either business banking or residential mortgage customers. Building a reputation as a digital first banking provider could be more challenging.

1: Direct, plan and improve key concepts

> How would you advise Banksbest to work towards this goal? What measures could Banksbest use to assess whether it has achieved its target? (Chapter 6 contains more detail about DPI, Measurement and Reporting that might help you here if you need a starting point).

Tactics describe the methods that will be used to enact a strategy. Tactics will be measured and may be changed or rejected if they are not delivering the required results. Tactical planning is often supported by standardised project and initiative planning within an organisation, whether it works in a waterfall or an Agile way. Plans need to address areas including dependencies, resources, costs and risks.

Operational work needs to be aligned to the organisation's strategy and tactics. **Operation** defines *"the routine running and management of an activity, product, service or other configuration item"*.

Operations usually includes predictable, documented, repeated tasks. It can also include managing more unusual situations. Operational procedures need to be communicated clearly to relevant staff, and standard methods and techniques defined where appropriate.

> Strategic, tactical and operational plans all need to be aligned. Incongruence describes the situation where elements do not agree with each other or are not

1: Direct, plan and improve key concepts

> compatible. I've experienced this feeling of incongruence in organisations between the strategic, tactical and operational levels. For example, one organisation held an annual strategy 'away day' attended by senior managers only. They developed what they felt was an appropriate approach for the next 12 months based on their desired outcomes and experiences. The resulting strategy was usually flawed for two main reasons:
>
> 1. The senior management team did not have a full view of the organisation, so its desired outcomes weren't always achievable.
> 2. The results of the away day weren't well communicated, so they weren't translated into tactical and operational activities.
>
> Each year, at the subsequent away day, lack of progress was blamed on poor employee engagement, rather than any failures in how the strategy itself was developed. It sounds basic and obvious, but many organisations still get simple things wrong, even with the best of intentions. Whatever level of the organisation you work at – strategic, tactical or operational – make sure you have a view of what is happening and what should be happening in the other levels.

Governance, compliance and management

Governance is *"the means by which an organization is directed and controlled"*. A governing body could be a person, or a group, accountable for performance and compliance. Governance includes:

- Establishing policies and monitoring their implementation; and

1: Direct, plan and improve key concepts

- Evaluating, directing and monitoring organisational activities (including those of service management).

> What policies exist in your organisation? Are you aware of them? Are policies followed, or circumvented?
>
> For those working in the operational levels of an organisation, the governing body may seem very remote and disconnected from day-to-day work. It's essential for everyone in the organisation to understand its overall direction. Every decision that is made must ultimately help the organisation get to where it needs to be.
>
> For example, imagine you're dealing with a very unhappy customer who wants a refund. What decisions are you allowed to make? How much autonomy do you have? What does your company value more: the customer's goodwill, or their payment? Without knowing the answer to these questions, you can't respond appropriately in this situation.

Compliance is *"both the act and result of ensuring that a standard or set of guidelines is followed, or that proper, consistent accounting or other practices are being employed"*. Effective governance includes compliance with applicable laws and regulations. Governance mechanisms ensure compliance with established policies.

1: Direct, plan and improve key concepts

Management is *"coordinated activities to define, control, supervise, and improve something"*. Management should be aligned with the directions from the governing body. Good management can lead to engaged employees, achievement of objectives, and efficient and effective operational activity.

> In many of the organisations that I've worked with, management responsibility is given to employees automatically after they have worked there for a certain time. Their knowledge of how things are done in the organisation will grow (hopefully!) along with their experience, so a progression to a management role seems like a logical step. But...is everyone suited to being a manager? If you were hired as the best engineer, or the best business analyst, that doesn't automatically mean that you will be the best manager.
>
> Good management leads to good results for the organisation overall. Poor management can lead to missed targets, crashing morale and good people leaving.
>
> Take a look at where managers come from in your organisation. Do career paths allow people to develop in a way that suits them, or are they automatically put into management roles? Back when I started my career, the organisation I worked with had two 'streams' – did you want to be in service management, or technology? For someone who was progressing from a service desk role, this was a significant decision that could set the course for

1: Direct, plan and improve key concepts

> their whole career. Looking back now, the distinction between what was seen as a process or a technical role seems very artificial.

Policies, controls and guidelines

Most organisations will have policies and guidelines in place. Policies provide strong (often mandatory) guidance, and guidelines offer more scope for creativity. An organisation's governance function will define policies and guidelines, and when each one is appropriate.

A **policy** is used to direct decisions and behaviour. Failing to follow a policy (for example, about sharing a password) can lead to disciplinary action. A policy is defined as *"formally documented management expectations and intentions, used to direct decisions and activities"*.

Policies are used to avoid an undesirable outcome or create a desirable outcome.

> From the Banksbest case study in the Appendix, you learned that "there is some conflict during board meetings, as the CFO is not fully convinced about the value of the CDO role and the digital transformation program. She would prefer to focus on cost management."
>
> Policies are set by the organisation's governance function, in this case, the board of directors. Put yourself in Lucy Jones's place for a second. Lucy is the product owner for My Way,

1: Direct, plan and improve key concepts

> which has three months before its next decision point relating to funding.
>
> Lucy reports to the CDO and is working on a project related to the digital transformation programme. She will also be aware that the CFO is not a champion of her project. The CFO has expectations related to cost management, not investment. Conflicting signals from the board will make Lucy's job more challenging and will make it harder for her to prioritise what needs to be done.

Guidelines provide guidance or recommendations but are not usually mandatory. A guideline is *"a recommended practice that allows some discretion in its interpretation, implementation or use"*. They can help staff understand how to behave in different situations, or when no particular policy applies.

> Rigid, control-based organisations often try to create a policy or control for every situation. Everything is documented, for every scenario: "If the customer does xx, you do yy. If the customer says zz, you say bb."
>
> This removes autonomy from the people actually carrying out the work and can reduce staff morale. It can also lead to frustrated customers who feel they are dealing with an automaton, not a person. Some of the most successful organisations I've worked with are the ones that give their

1: Direct, plan and improve key concepts

> staff guidelines to work within, with clearly defined outcomes. Telling staff that you want them to do whatever is in their power to make the customer happy allows them to get creative, and to work with the customer to reach a shared solution. Sometimes the best solution is counterintuitive. For example, one organisation had a service level agreement (SLA) that said that an engineer would be on site to address a printer failure within 24 hours. In one instance, although the repair was urgent, the customer wasn't going to be available, so extending the target and arranging the visit after 48 hours delivered a much better outcome. The happy customer was worth more to the service provider than unthinkingly following the SLA.

Controls are *"the means of managing a risk, ensuring that a business objective is achieved, or that a process is followed"*. Organisations will use policies, controls and guidelines to help them deliver their desired outcomes and co-create value with customers.

Value, outcomes, costs and risks

ITIL 4 describes how value calculations need to include outcomes, costs and risks. Service providers help consumers achieve desired outcomes by deploying their resources and taking on some of the costs and risks of service provision. Service consumers assess what costs and risks are removed and added by using a product or service.

Each service provider organisation will define its desired outcomes and analyse the costs and risks associated with them. These outcomes are then achieved through clear direction, planning and improvement. The service portfolio will evolve as the strategy evolves.

Figure 1: Considering outcomes, costs and risks to achieve value[1]

---

[1] *ITIL® 4: Direct, Plan and Improve*, figure 1.2. Copyright © AXELOS Limited 2020. Used under permission of AXELOS Limited. All rights reserved.

CHAPTER 2: DPI SCOPE, KEY PRINCIPLES AND METHODS

This chapter studies the scope of control in more depth, including:

- How to cascade objectives and requirements;
- How to define effective policies, controls and guidelines; and
- How to place decision-making authority at the correct level.

Cascading objectives

The dictionary definition of objective is "a thing aimed at or sought; a goal."

Once the organisation's mission and strategy are defined, they can be used to create and cascade objectives. Objectives are used to translate the strategy through the organisational levels, ensuring they stay aligned. Organisations create feedback loops by reporting on the achievement of objectives.

Figure 2 shows an example of an objectives cascade.

2: DPI scope, key principles and methods

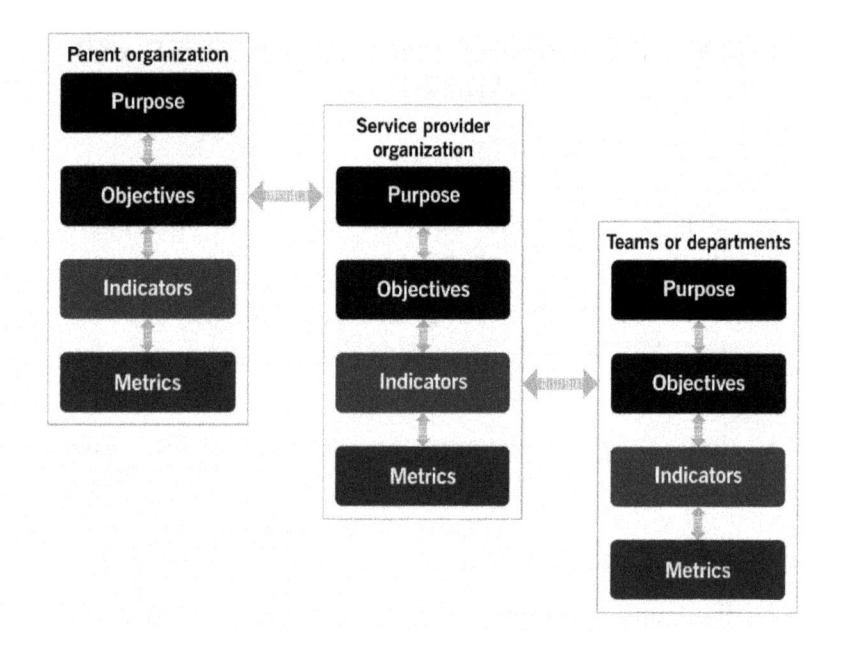

Figure 2: An example of an objectives cascade[2]

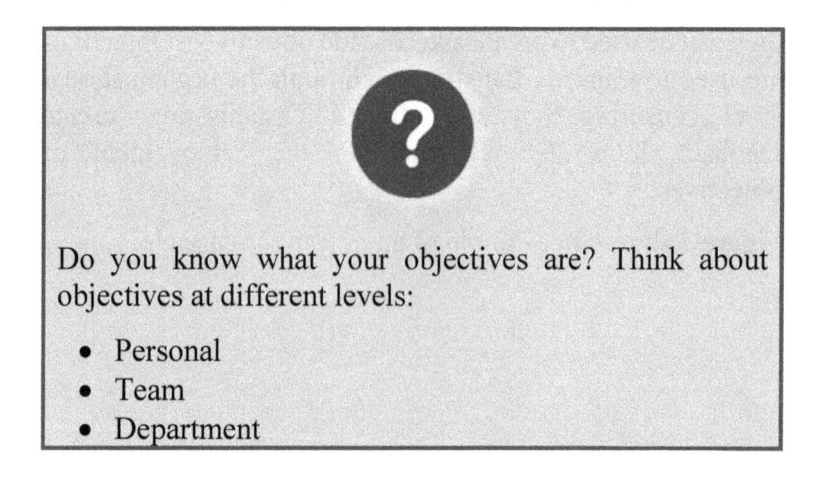

Do you know what your objectives are? Think about objectives at different levels:

- Personal
- Team
- Department

---

[2] *ITIL® 4: Direct, Plan and Improve*, figure 2.1. Copyright © AXELOS Limited 2020.

2: DPI scope, key principles and methods

> - Organisation
>
> Have you been involved in setting any of the objectives that apply to your role? If not, what is the impact of that? If you work in a management role, does your team understand its objectives?

Cascading requirements

Objectives and plans are cascaded through the organisation. Information about the resource requirements needed to achieve them also needs to be cascaded through the organisation. Figure 3 shows how resource requirements could relate to any of the four service management dimensions.

2: DPI scope, key principles and methods

Organizations and people

Partners and suppliers

Strategy

Information and technology

Value streams and processes

Figure 3: Four-dimension requirements for fulfilling a strategy[3]

Decision-making

Decisions need to be made at the right level of the organisation. Typically, governance decisions take place at the highest level, but then other decisions should be delegated as far as possible. This relates to the scope of

---

[3] *ITIL® 4: Direct, Plan and Improve*, figure 2.2. Copyright © AXELOS Limited 2020.

2: DPI scope, key principles and methods

control for each role within the organisation. If employees have a very broad scope of control, there is a risk that they might inadvertently make harmful decisions. If they don't have a wide enough scope of control, every decision has to be escalated, wasting valuable time and energy.

If employees have a very narrow scope of control, they may feel unmotivated and powerless. This can lead to low productivity, and a reluctance to take on new responsibilities. Risk management can be used to help decide how decisions should be made. High-risk decisions need to be made in a way that allows for structure, audit trail and review. Low-risk decisions can be delegated with less negative impact. Risk levels can be moderated with training, automation, policies and guidelines.

> Think about decision-making at Banksbest. Lucy Jones is the product owner for My Way, reporting to the CDO. The scope of the work includes testing biometrics, cheque pay-in functionality and customer feedback monitoring. My Way is meant to allow business banking customers to use a range of devices to manage their accounts, and supports the strategic goals related to growing business banking customers and Banksbest being seen as a digital first banking provider.
>
> Working with the digital team, Lucy will be involved in decision-making every day. These decisions will relate to features, technology and prioritisation, among many other

> considerations. Lucy's scope of control should allow her to make these decisions without constantly consulting the CDO.
>
> If Lucy is required to make a decision that could have an impact on the achievement of the strategic goals (for example: implementing this functionality would make our existing business banking customers happy, but won't attract any new customers), she could consult the CDO for advice.
>
> Devolved decision-making should allow staff to feel empowered. It should not lead to staff feeling scared about making decisions that are beyond their capabilities or their scope of control. Managers need to work with staff and identify any improvement opportunities related to decision-making.

Defining effective policies, controls and guidelines

Policies, controls and guidelines need to have meaning. If staff can't understand why each one exists, they are much less likely to follow them.

Policies form part of an organisation's control landscape. Staff need to be able to provide feedback on policies, including complaints about them or suggestions for improvement. This feedback should be assessed, and any actions taken as a result should be communicated to relevant stakeholders.

Organisations introduce **controls** to deliver a desired result. They also use them to avoid any unintended undesirable consequences. Controls need to be regularly reviewed to ensure they are effective and are delivering the results they

2: DPI scope, key principles and methods

are meant to. Many controls are implemented through measurements and reports.

The data collected through measurements and reports needs to be valid and relevant. Many organisations measure too much and lose sight of what is actually important. The ITIL guiding principle 'focus on value' can be used as a guide to help simplify measurement and reporting. Where possible, controls should be automated to reduce the resources required to manage them, and to standardise their reporting.

> In my experience, controls multiply over time. When something goes wrong, a new control is put in place to try to prevent recurrence. For example, a change to a piece of software failed because of an undocumented dependency. New rules are applied to all future changes to try to identify this type of dependency, even though the check isn't relevant or necessary for the vast majority of changes. Gradually, the check becomes a 'tick box' exercise; the work isn't really carried out, but the forms are filled in.
>
> Controls need to be well understood and regularly reviewed. It can be challenging to get staff to admit that they aren't doing what they are supposed to do in order to meet the control requirements, so think about how you collect this type of information. Consider your own role, and any controls that you do or don't follow.

2: DPI scope, key principles and methods

Guidelines are recommendations, not mandatory. They don't have to be used, so their adoption relies on them being easy to access, understand and follow. The staff members who carry out a task, or have more experience in a particular role, are often best placed to define guidelines for carrying out the work. Guidelines also need to be regularly reviewed to ensure they are still relevant and accurate.

Guidelines aren't necessary for every task in an organisation. They are particularly valuable for tasks that:

- Are performed by many people, or in a team with high staff turnover;
- Used to be performed in a different way, or seem confusing at first;
- Are performed infrequently but need to be done consistently; and
- Can be done quicker or better with guidance.

Policies, controls and guidelines are only effective when they are used. Documenting them is not enough. Involving people in the definition of policies, controls and guidelines can help ensure staff feel ownership and involvement from the start. Clearly communicating why these elements exist and providing education (for example, during staff induction) help increase their usage. Staff also need to see managers following policies. If policies are 'just for show' or only followed by certain people, they will not be fully adopted.

CHAPTER 3: THE ROLE OF GOVERNANCE, RISK AND COMPLIANCE

Risk management is an important part of direction, planning and improvement. No organisation is immune to risk. Risks need to be managed to increase the chance of an organisation meeting its objectives. Direction must consider risk; plans must address risk; improvements need to consider risk.

> Is someone responsible for risk management in your organisation? Are you aware of a risk register for your team, your product or the organisation as a whole? How would you report a risk that you became aware of? If you can't answer these questions, that is a risk in its own right!

Risks and controls

Risk is *"a possible event that could cause harm or loss or make it more difficult to achieve objectives. It can also be defined as uncertainty of outcome and can be used in the context of measuring the probability of positive outcomes as well as negative outcomes."*

A control is *"the means of managing a risk, ensuring that a business objective is achieved, or that a process is followed"*.

3: The role of governance, risk and compliance

Risk and direction

Risk management isn't a one-off exercise. It must be applied continually, at all levels of the organisation.

Table 1: Continual Risk Management

Long-term objectives and risk management	Long-term objectives relate to strategic decisions, setting the context for decision-making at other levels. Risk management considerations might include definition of the organisation's risk appetite and risk thresholds. How much risk is the organisation prepared to deal with? Strategic risks may not have any impact for weeks or even months, so they need to be reviewed regularly. Portfolio management has a role to play here, looking at risks to products and services.
Medium-term objectives and risk management	Medium-term objectives normally relate to the product portfolio, and programmes and projects used to deliver business change. The decision scope is narrower, and timescales

3: The role of governance, risk and compliance

	are shorter than at the strategic level. Risks may create an impact more quickly, so they may be managed sooner.
Short-term objectives and risk management	Short-term objectives relate to the operational level. Risk management decisions made here need to be aligned with long- and medium-term objectives.

Figure 4[4] shows the interaction between long-, medium- and short-term objectives.

---

[4] *ITIL® 4: Direct, Plan and Improve*, figure 2.3. Copyright © AXELOS Limited 2020.

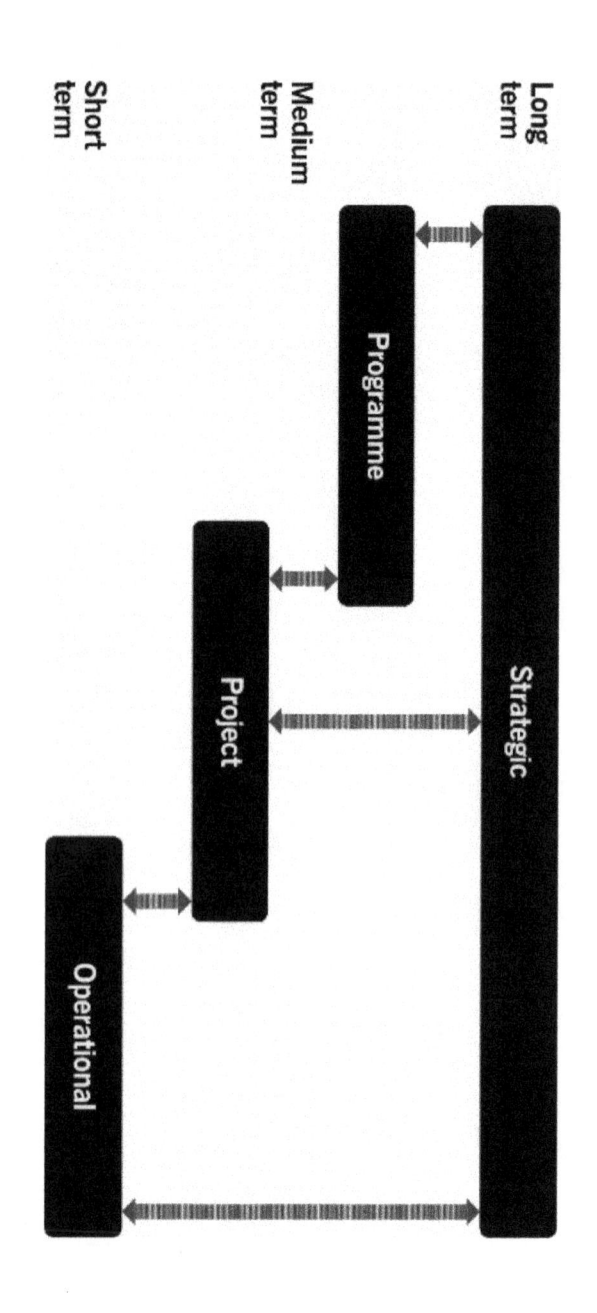

Figure 4: Interactions between long-, medium-, and short-term objectives

3: The role of governance, risk and compliance

The most common failing I see in an organisation's approach to risk management is inconsistency. This happens in two main ways. First, some organisations focus a lot of attention on a risk management exercise, and then allow all the work that has been done to be wasted. This typically happens when a risk management workshop is held and risks are documented, but there is no role accountable for measuring progress or keeping the risk register up to date.

Second, I see inconsistency in the approach to risk management at different levels of the organisation. It's critical that all levels are aligned. For example, if the long-term strategic view is that security is fundamental to the survival of the organisation, it's not acceptable to have operational teams sharing passwords and lending each other their access cards to get in and out of the building. Vertical consistency throughout the organisation is necessary for effective risk management.

3: The role of governance, risk and compliance

How difficult does risk management need to be? Put simply, not difficult at all! Consider a simple risk register and the information you need:

- Risk number or unique identifier.
- Date raised.
- Raised by.
- Risk and impact description.
- Probability score (1–3).
- Impact score (1–3).
- Overall risk score based on probability x impact.
- Owner.
- Date of last update.
- Status (open/closed/etc.).

Once you have this information, you can create a mitigation plan and rescore the probability and impact based on the mitigating factors being applied.

For example, at Banksbest, Doug Range might identify a risk that the quality of service in the customer service centre falls because staff don't have enough knowledge about the My Way product. This might be given an impact and probability score of 2 and 2, based on previous experience, giving an overall risk score of 4. The mitigating action might be for Doug and Lucy to work closely together, allowing Doug to gain insight into My

3: The role of governance, risk and compliance

> Way and prepare training materials for the customer service staff.

Everyone in the organisation has a role to play in risk management. Staff should feel safe to report risks and know that their information will be acted on if appropriate. Direction, guidance and support can be provided so that people know what risks can be tolerated and what needs escalation.

Risk and improvement

Every plan needs to assess the risks associated with it. If the risks are too great, the plan may be terminated. Improvement plans also need to apply risk management principles. For any improvement, consider the risk of making the improvement, but also the risk of not doing anything. Each organisation has its own level of risk that can be tolerated.

DPI and governance

There is a strong relationship between direction, planning and improvement, and governance. The areas considered in the DPI syllabus include:

- Governance structures used for decision-making;
- Governance of the service provider;
- Placing decision-making at the right level;
- Impacts of governance on DPI; and
- How to ensure controls are sufficient but not excessive.

An organisation's decisions must align with its mission and strategy. It will use different structures and methods to

3: The role of governance, risk and compliance

support decision-making and direction of activity and behaviours.

Governance structures

An organisation might not use all the structures defined, but the roles should be fulfilled.

Table 2: Governance Structures

Board of directors	The board of directors is responsible for the organisation's governance, including: *"Setting strategic objectives* *Providing leadership to implement strategy* *Supervising management* *Reporting to shareholders"*
Shareholders	Shareholders are responsible for appointing directors and auditors to ensure effective governance.
Audit committee	The audit committee supports the board of directors by providing independent assessment of

3: The role of governance, risk and compliance

	management performance and conformance.

The governance structures supply directives, which then define internal controls. Controls can include:

- Risk management;
- Compliance controls;
- Operational controls;
- Financial controls; and
- Any others required.

The board will review risk management systems and internal control systems at least annually.

Governance of the service provider

If a service provider is an organisation, it will have its own governance structures. If the service provider is part of a larger organisation (for example, an IT department in a business), the parent organisation will have governing authority over it. Authority and governance can be delegated to lower levels, but the organisation's governing body must still oversee governance.

The ITIL service value system (SVS) can be applied to the entire organisation or to a department or departments. If the SVS is used at departmental level, governance must be aligned with organisational governance. Applicable external legislation and regulations also need to be continually reviewed and integrated where necessary, for example Sarbanes-Oxley or the General Data Protection Regulation (GDPR).

3: The role of governance, risk and compliance

Placing decision-making at the right level

Governors should review decision-making for the organisation and identify where decisions could be delegated. Equally, if there has been negative impact related to delegated decisions, the scope of control may need to change. This should be considered as an improvement exercise, rather than an opportunity to assign blame.

DPI and governance are closely related. **Direction** from the governing body affects the whole organisation. Employees will struggle if they are asked to carry out activities that are in conflict with overall organisational direction. Governance decisions and directives are inputs to planning at all levels. **Plans** may be used to deliver compliance or governance objectives. **Improvement** initiatives should increase the organisation's compliance with its directives.

Ensuring controls are sufficient but not excessive

Effective controls provide 'just enough' control. Too much, and outcomes might be negatively affected; too little, and risk is created. Controls need to be designed carefully – reinforced by the guiding principle 'focus on value'.

Measurements are often used as controls. Where this is the case:

- Consider avoiding unnecessary or excessive measurements;
- Consider focusing on value to measure what is important; and
- Remember that measuring people can change how they behave.

3: The role of governance, risk and compliance

Have you ever changed your behaviour because you knew it was being measured? Did the measurements lead to better behaviour, or worse? Think about how you would drive your car if you had a driving examiner sat next to you – what would you change? Why?

When using measures as part of a suite of controls, many organisations now focus on **outcomes** they are trying to achieve (for example, keeping customer data secure), rather than outputs (for example, the number of security patches applied, the volume of information sent to customers with guides to setting passwords, etc.). Measuring outcomes can be challenging as they are more difficult to quantify, but they allow the measurements to express the intent of the control. If an organisation only measures outputs or activities, it can be easy to miss the bigger picture.

CHAPTER 4: FOCUS ON IMPROVEMENT

The DPI syllabus looks at all aspects of continual improvement and the use of the ITIL 4 continual improvement model. The topics covered in this chapter include:

- How to use the continual improvement model in relation to the service value system (SVS);
- How to identify assessment objectives, outputs, requirements and criteria;
- How to select an appropriate assessment method;
- How to define and prioritise improvement outcomes;
- How to build, justify and advocate for a business case;
- How to conduct improvement reviews and analyse lessons learned; and
- How to embed continual improvement in the SVS.

Creating a continual improvement culture

Improvements are changes and can affect an organisation's culture. They need to be managed accordingly. Creating an improvement culture will have a more sustained impact than a series of disconnected improvement initiatives.

A culture of improvement is supported by a governance capability that provides leadership, management and resources. The improvement practice itself will be subject to continual improvement.

An improvement culture should lead to small, incremental improvements. This will have less negative or disruptive

4: Focus on improvement

impact on the organisation than a single huge improvement that affects all the four dimensions of service management.

> "But we've always done it that way!"
>
> "We tried that before, it didn't work!"
>
> Do you recognise this type of response? What is blocking improvement in your organisation? What needs to happen for improvement ideas to flow more freely?

> I've worked with a couple of organisations that struggled with their improvement culture because of low staff turnover. High staff turnover is usually seen as a danger sign, but these organisations were experiencing the opposite. People stayed for 20+ years, and some of them were counting down the days until retirement. The organisations suffered due to cultural inertia, a feeling that everything had already been tried, and a lack of new perspectives.
>
> To address this situation, you could look at bringing in some external resources such as consultants, but I still

4: Focus on improvement

> believe it's better to identify improvements from inside the organisation. Consider:
> - Encouraging staff to attend external events and meetups (face-to-face or virtual) where they will be exposed to new ideas from different organisations; and
> - Creating incentives for improvements (these can be formal or informal, depending on the overall organisational culture and reward mechanisms in place).

Continual improvement of the service value chain and practices

The service value chain (SVC) activities can be combined in any order to create value streams. Improvements can be applied to the individual activities, or to the entire value chain and value streams. If a single activity is being improved, the impact on the overall SVC must be understood. Are there any dependencies?

ITIL practices also contribute to the SVC. If a practice isn't performing as it is intended to, this will have an impact on the value chain and associated value streams. Practices also need to be subject to review and improvement.

> There's no worse feeling than making a change or improvement and realising you've inadvertently broken

4: Focus on improvement

> something somewhere else. Do you have a good view of the dependencies related to your work? How can you discover and visualise them? Building views of dependencies can also be a great way to build relationships across teams and allow joint improvement ideas to surface.

Continual improvement in organisations

An improvement programme is not a one-time exercise for an organisation. When an improvement has been made, it's then time to look for the next improvement opportunity. The organisation itself will be evolving over time, as its strategy, market, consumers, etc. change. This evolution will also give rise to new improvement opportunities and initiatives. Continual improvement should be seen as an integral part of every role in the organisation.

"The continual improvement practice aligns an organization's practices and services with changing business needs through the ongoing improvement of products, services, practices, and the management of products and services."

Improvements can be implemented at every level – from an individual and their own activities to the whole organisation. Each staff member should understand how to progress an improvement opportunity.

Creating an improvement culture and integrating improvement into every role in the organisation will ensure that continual improvement isn't forgotten or seen as low priority. Once the context for improvement is in place, continual improvement techniques and methods can be used

4: Focus on improvement

to track, prioritise, implement and measure improvement initiatives.

The continual improvement model

Using a defined model for continual improvement means initiatives are more likely to be successful. The model provides a path to follow. The ITIL continual improvement model focuses on consumer value, and ensures all initiatives are linked back to the overall business vision. The model can be adapted to meet organisational requirements and is suitable for use in both Agile and waterfall environments.

4: Focus on improvement

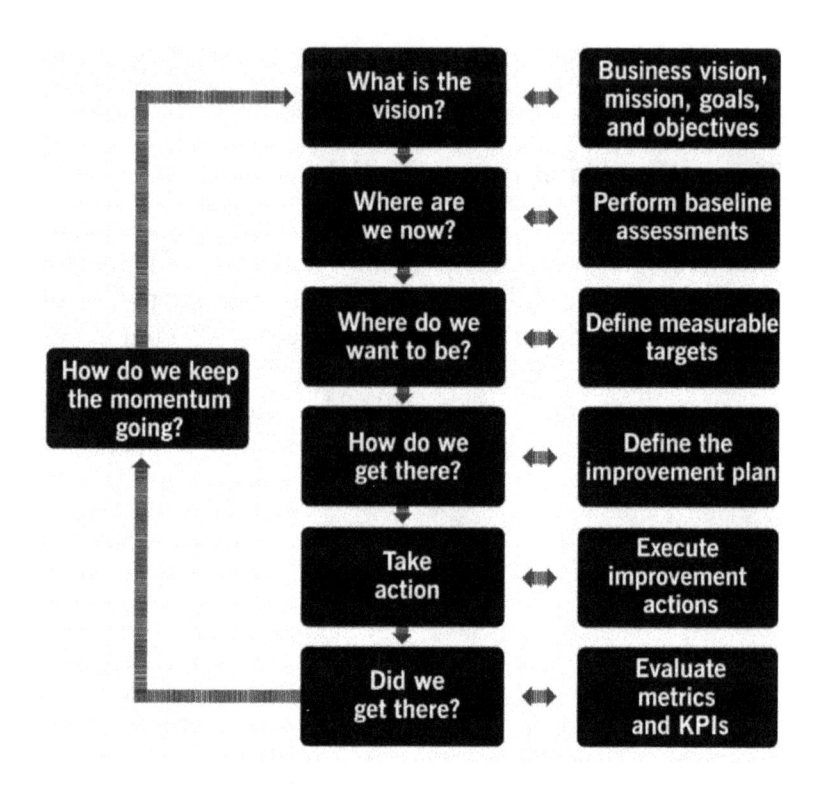

```
What is the vision?  ⇔  Business vision, mission, goals, and objectives
        ↓
Where are we now?  ⇔  Perform baseline assessments
        ↓
Where do we want to be?  ⇔  Define measurable targets
        ↓                                            How do we keep the momentum going?
How do we get there?  ⇔  Define the improvement plan
        ↓
Take action  ⇔  Execute improvement actions
        ↓
Did we get there?  ⇔  Evaluate metrics and KPIs
```

Figure 5: The continual improvement model[5]

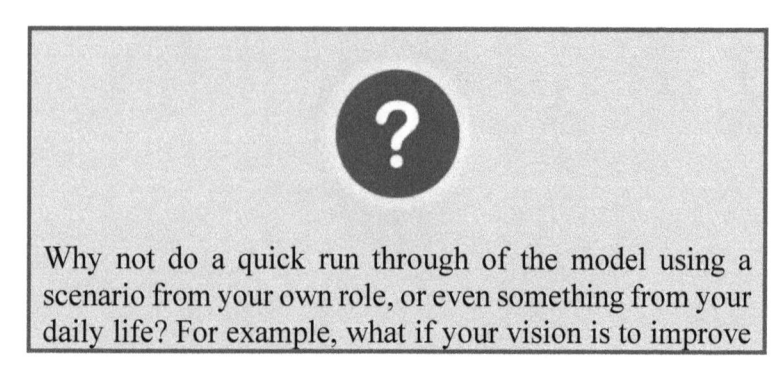

> Why not do a quick run through of the model using a scenario from your own role, or even something from your daily life? For example, what if your vision is to improve

---

[5] *ITIL® 4: Direct, Plan and Improve*, figure 0.3. Copyright © AXELOS Limited 2020.

4: Focus on improvement

> your health? You can assess your current state and look at mental health, diet, exercise, and how you know that changes are working. If you've ever tried to change your diet and given up too quickly, you'll know how important it is to measure progress and to keep momentum going. You might also know what it's like to change everything at once (diet, sleep, exercise, alcohol consumption) ...and then not know which change has delivered any positive results you experience.

Step 1 – What is the vision?

Individual improvement initiatives need to be aligned with the organisation's overall objectives. The improvement initiative also needs a clear vision of what it will deliver. Improvement initiatives need to be regularly reassessed to ensure they are still aligned with the organisation's overall vision and strategy.

At the end of this step, change agents should have a high-level vision for an improvement, including:

- Agreed high-level direction;
- Description, including the vision and the change agent's scope of control;
- An understanding of relevant stakeholders and their role; and
- The expected value.

4: Focus on improvement

> **?**
>
> Banksbest has a strategic goal to grow its residential mortgage business by 50%. Go through the continual improvement model from Banksbest's perspective and consider what actions it might take. Can this goal be aligned with the other strategic goal of being seen as a 'digital first' organisation? Are there some actions that could support both goals? For example, online mortgage applications and using artificial intelligence to support credit checking might help support both goals. If there is legislation that requires paper forms to be filled in and signatures to be witnessed and notarised, these actions won't support the digital first goal.

Change agents can be a business unit, department, team and/or an individual. They must understand how the organisation's vision, mission and objectives relate to the improvement(s) they are acting as the change agent for.

An improvement initiative could be suggested via the continual improvement register, meeting actions, management directives, development logs, problem records or other sources. Alternatively, change agents could target an area of the organisation where they know improvement is possible. Creating a holistic shared vision for improvement is more effective than having a vision based on the view of a small group.

4: Focus on improvement

> The idea of a shared vision for improvement is absolutely critical. It's important for organisations to document initiatives on some type of improvement register, but the *idea* of improvement also needs to be something that lives and breathes in the organisation. Improvement initiatives need to be reviewed, discussed and continually refined. As priorities change, the importance of improvements will also change. These discussions can take place formally at scheduled meetings, etc., but why not also create space for informal discussion? My organisation has an 'experiments' channel in Slack (other collaboration tools are available!) where we can all suggest changes based on our own activities and what we notice in the organisation. Small changes are often done immediately and then monitored; other ideas might be carried forward for discussion in the team meeting.

Anyone in the organisation can have a vision for improvement, within their own scope of control. This needs to align with the organisational vision. All improvement initiatives should have:

- Clear objectives that communicate intent;
- A description of expected value;
- Direction;
- Desired future state; and
- Criteria for success.

4: Focus on improvement

Step 2 – Where are we now?

If we don't know where we are right now, it's very hard to map what we need to do to get to our desired future state. Current state metrics can be used to provide an objective measure of the current position.

By the end of step 2, change agents should have:

- A clear understanding of the current state of the area for improvement; and
- Baseline measurements and metrics of the current state to be used for comparison. A baseline is a minimum or starting point used for comparisons.

Assessments are used to measure, analyse and understand. Processes, services, technology, organisational culture and people can all be assessed, and their behaviour and performance studied. An assessment shows what is being done well, and where there are gaps and issues. (There is more information on assessments later in this chapter).

Step 3 – Where do we want to be?

Once the current state is understood, change agents can plan for the desired future state. The 'next' state may not be perfect; it may be a small improvement on what exists now, with further improvements planned once that state is reached. Small, iterative improvements are more likely to be successful than dramatic, far-reaching changes that can seem overwhelming. Once the desired outcomes have been defined, they can be scoped and prioritised. Some outcomes may have higher value than others, and there may be dependencies that mean activities have to take place in a specific order.

4: Focus on improvement

> Having run my own business for 13 years, I've already made a lot of mistakes relating to improvements (although I'm sure there will be more mistakes to come as well). We're on about the eighth version of our website at my training business, and new websites have been a major source of learning for us. Early on, we never made incremental changes. We'd have an imperfect website live while we struggled in the background to build something perfect. Eventually, a deadline (often a technology change) would force us to release the new site and we would have to suffer through a huge disruption that resulted in another imperfect website. We were making multiple errors – focusing on 'a new site' rather than the outcomes we wanted, making too many changes at the same time and letting the deadline drive the project. Now, we try to make smaller changes to the existing site, allowing each improvement to settle in and giving us time to measure the results.

Prioritisation criteria need to be transparent and impartial. If there is any question or debate about correct prioritisation, a governance committee can provide support and act as an escalation point. Sometimes, low-cost, low-effort improvements will be implemented first to deliver rapid value. This can create momentum and help stakeholders see the benefit of investing in higher-cost, more complex initiatives.

4: Focus on improvement

A business case may be needed during this step. The business case will need to be agreed by the change agents and the stakeholders who will authorise budget and resources. (There is more information about business cases later in this chapter.)

Step 4 – How do we get there?

Once the desired future state is understood, change agents can prepare an action plan, which will answer these questions:

- *"Do any of the changes need to be completed in a specific order?*
- *Are there any quick wins that can be delivered early to give rapid customer value?*
- *Are there any resourcing constraints that will dictate the flow of changes?"*

If any new information is revealed, earlier steps in the model may need to be revisited.

By the time step 4 is complete, the change agents should have:

- An approved action plan; and
- An understanding of the nature of the improvements and the most efficient way to deliver them.

Any plan needs to comply with organisational policies and use any required templates or tools. The plan should contain just enough information to support the desired outcomes; planning activity should be efficient and lightweight.

The plan needs to address how feedback and metrics will be collected and used. Some organisations have developed a

4: Focus on improvement

habit of following their instinct and making improvements based on 'gut feel', perception or subjective data. Without a clear understanding of their start point, the actions taken and the results, it can be very challenging to show the value of an improvement initiative.

A continual improvement culture will deliver small improvements on an ongoing basis. This allows results to be measured and plans to be adjusted based on the value delivered. If there isn't enough information to create a plan, experiments can be used to test hypotheses instead, allowing an option to be selected. This is a more Agile approach to improvement.

> Think about where Banksbest should start with its improvement initiatives. Mibank has the potential to attract new customers and increase the satisfaction of existing ones. But Bizbank is in use by client-facing teams and isn't always operating as well as it should. Would it be better to spend some time and effort here to ensure existing customers are happy?

Step 5 – Take action

Once the plan is complete, action begins. The plan will be assessed and revised if necessary, as actions are completed, and experiments carried out. By the end of step 5, change agents should have completed the planned actions from the previous step. There may be several action plans running in

4: Focus on improvement

parallel. Links and dependencies between plans also need to be managed.

Step 6 – Did we get there?

Step 6 confirms that the action plan delivered the desired result(s). By the end of this step, change agents should have:

- Verified results based on data analysis; and
- A documented improvement review.

An improvement review is *"an evaluation using metrics and other evidence to determine whether an improvement has achieved its desired outcomes and, if not, what needs to be done to complete the work"*.

> I've seen many organisations launch improvement initiatives with great fanfare, only for them to gradually fizzle out. When they look back to see if they spent their money wisely, it's hard to tell if the improvement delivered any tangible results. My advice would be to design the metrics at the same time as you design the improvement. Don't realise too late that you don't have the ability to assess whether or not your work has been successful.

4: Focus on improvement

Step 7 – How do we keep momentum going?

Improvement is never finished. Successful initiatives need to be publicised and marketed to reinforce the changes and keep momentum going for future improvements.

At the end of this step, the change agents should have:

- Confirmation that improvements are established;
- Recommendations for future improvements and improvement iterations; and
- A documented lessons-learned analysis for future improvement initiatives.

Assessments

There are three main types of assessment, shown in Table 3:

Table 3: Types of Assessment

Qualitative	*"Leveraging the assessor's knowledge and experience, qualitative assessments are opinion-driven and are therefore subject to interpretation. Self-assessments are primarily qualitative."*
Quantitative	*"Quantitative assessments are evidence-oriented and are therefore more objective; these assessments rely on accurate, complete data.*

4: Focus on improvement

	Formal audits are typically quantitative."
Hybrid	*"A combination of qualitative and quantitative, hybrid assessments involve experts analyzing evidence and giving their opinions. Assessments used for identifying and implementing improvements are usually most effective when they employ a hybrid approach."*

It's a good idea to use a mixture of quantitative and qualitative assessments. Qualitative assessments such as a customer satisfaction survey often attract extremes of opinion – the respondent either loved or hated the product or service. These opinions can then be balanced alongside the quantitative results – for example, 95% of our customers said they loved their restaurant meal, but we had a 20% return rate for food being sent back to the kitchen. How do we balance these pieces of information?

4: Focus on improvement

Assessment objectives need to be defined and documented. The objectives can then be shared with stakeholders to support their understanding of the assessment. Assessments can be one-off or regular activities, and occur before, during and after improvement initiatives.

Example assessment objectives could include:

- Understanding how well something is performing;
- Establishing baselines before improvement activities;
- Understanding if an improvement met its objectives;
- Comparing an organisation with another similar or competing organisation; and
- Understanding any gaps or changes needed to comply with a standard.

DPI provides examples of seven different assessment types, summarised in Table 4:

4: Focus on improvement

Table 4: Assessment Methods and their Outputs[6]

Assessment method	Output
Gap analysis	*Identification of the differences between actual practice and the chosen assessment criteria.*
SWOT analysis	*Identification of strengths, weaknesses, opportunities, and threats.*
Change readiness assessment	*An estimation of the organization's ability to transition to a new way of working.*
Customer/user satisfaction analysis	*Analysis of how customers and/or users feel about the services they use, based on their feedback.*
SLA achievement analysis	*Analysis of the quality of a service or services based on a comparison of service performance against*

---

[6] *ITIL® 4: Direct, Plan and Improve*, table 3.8. Copyright © AXELOS Limited 2020.

4: Focus on improvement

	service level agreement (SLA) targets.
Benchmarking	*A comparison of the results of this assessment with the results of similar assessments performed for other comparable organizations.*
Maturity assessment	*An estimation of the maturity of a process or an organization based on a defined framework, such as the ITIL process maturity model.*

> Unless assessments already take place regularly in your organisation, remember that being part of an assessment can be worrying for people. Be very clear about why assessments are taking place, and what will happen to the assessment findings. If people feel stressed about an assessment, they are more likely to tell you what they think you want to hear, rather than the truth. This can mean improvement opportunities are missed.

> One organisation I worked with regularly went through job evaluation assessments. Staff were asked to document their roles and day-to-day activities. They knew that the assessment could lead to their role being downgraded (or even being made redundant), so the assessment inputs were fabulous works of fiction and didn't support any meaningful actions.

Assessment method 1 – Gap analysis

Gap analysis compares the current state with a desired future state and highlights the nature and scope of the gap between them. This gap is sometimes referred to as the 'delta'. The gap will change as the desired future state changes, so gap analysis is an ongoing activity.

The 'delta' can be understood by considering:

- Where the organisation is now;
- The desired future state;
- Where competitors are, or are moving towards; and
- Where customers want the organisation to be.

Table 5 outlines some of the pros and cons of gap analysis:

4: Focus on improvement

Table 5: Pros and Cons of Gap Analysis[7]

Pros	Cons
• It enables the documentation of customer experiences against customer expectations. • It provides a basis for prioritization. • It allows for the collection of productivity measures. • It documents product or service features that are accidentally left out or deliberately eliminated, or which require additional development. • It provides an active comparison of current activities with compliance requirements.	• A gap analysis is not an economical evaluation method. • Areas performing similar or duplicate functions may not be included in the scope of the analysis (e.g. incident response teams performing change management). • Interpreting the results is subjective.

---

[7] *ITIL® 4: Direct, Plan and Improve*, table 3.9. Copyright © AXELOS Limited 2020.

4: Focus on improvement

Assessment Method 2 – SWOT analysis

Figure 6[8] shows the areas considered during a SWOT analysis. SWOT looks at internal and external risks to an organisation, as well as how it differs from its competition or similar organisations.

Strengths and weaknesses are internal factors that affect how an organisation moves towards its objectives. Threats and opportunities are external to the organisation. This means they are outside of its control, but they still need to be considered during change and improvement planning.

SWOT is normally presented as a grid and can help an organisation exploit its strengths and minimise weaknesses. Opportunities can be seized, and threats mitigated. SWOT can be carried out at a personal, departmental or organisational level. It's most effective when carried out by a group, to get a broad range of inputs.

---

[8] *ITIL® 4: Direct, Plan and Improve*, figure 3.1. Copyright © AXELOS Limited 2020.

4: Focus on improvement

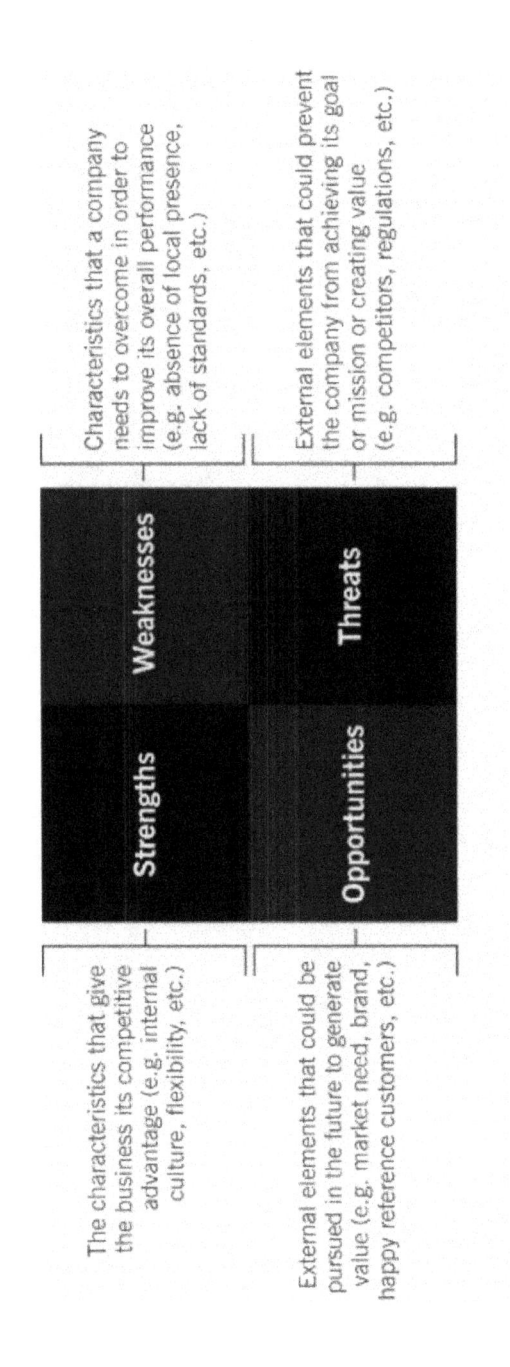

Strengths: The characteristics that give the business its competitive advantage (e.g. internal culture, flexibility, etc.)

Weaknesses: Characteristics that a company needs to overcome in order to improve its overall performance (e.g. absence of local presence, lack of standards, etc.)

Opportunities: External elements that could be pursued in the future to generate value (e.g. market need, brand, happy reference customers, etc.)

Threats: External elements that could prevent the company from achieving its goal or mission or creating value (e.g. competitors, regulations, etc.)

Figure 6: SWOT analysis

4: Focus on improvement

Table 6 outlines some of the pros and cons of SWOT analysis:

Table 6: Pros and Cons of SWOT Analysis[9]

Pros	Cons
• Can be swift to compile and deliver. • Provides focus at strategic, management, and operational levels supporting objectives. • Permits compartmentalization to enhance strengths and opportunities while addressing weaknesses and threats independently. • Follows the same process whether the subject is a strategy, business case, product, or service.	• Identifying and scheduling the right participants can be difficult and time-consuming. • SWOT analyses do not usually prioritize or weight the resulting lists. SWOT analyses are subjective.

---

[9] *ITIL® 4: Direct, Plan and Improve,* table 3.10. Copyright © AXELOS Limited 2020.

4: Focus on improvement

> Draw up a SWOT analysis for your organisation. Does it highlight any surprising information? Anything for immediate attention? Now try Banksbest – imagine it is a real organisation operating in the country you are in. How does its SWOT look for your region?

Assessment method 3 – Change readiness assessment

A change readiness assessment *"estimates an organization's preparedness to transition to a new way of working"*.

Understanding the organisation's level of readiness will help ensure a change is successful. Organisations that resist change are less likely to have a culture of continual improvement, and change will be more challenging to implement.

Table 7 outlines some of the pros and cons of change readiness assessment:

4: Focus on improvement

Table 7: Pros and Cons of Change Readiness Assessments[10]

Pros	Cons
• Allow change agents to address the human side of change with full awareness of where issues lie. *• Identify potential challenges before implementing change.* *• Increase the probability that changes will be implemented successfully and sustained.*	*• Change readiness assessments consider complex factors which may overwhelm assessors.* *• Employees' reactions to change readiness assessments are difficult to predict.* *• Change readiness models are numerous and subject to interpretation.* *• Identifying the obstacles to successful change does not mean the organization can or will address them.*

More information on organisational change management can be found in the ITIL 4 Practice Guide for this practice.

---

[10] *ITIL® 4: Direct, Plan and Improve*, table 3.11. Copyright © AXELOS Limited 2020.

4: Focus on improvement

> Change readiness assessments provide an important, holistic view of an organisation's readiness for change. Too often, change agents focus on technical readiness and miss the human elements.

Assessment Method 4 – Customer/user satisfaction analysis

If an improvement or a change was implemented to improve customer or user satisfaction levels, they will need to be measured before, during and after the improvement activity. For some services, the customer and the user are the same person. For other services, the roles are separate and will need to be measured individually.

Table 8 outlines some of the pros and cons of customer/user satisfaction analysis:

4: Focus on improvement

Table 8: Pros and Cons of Customer/User Satisfaction Analyses[11]

Pros	Cons
• *Provide insight on the value of products or services, and the faith customers and users have in the service provider's ability to meet its commitments.* • *Monitor the customer's and user's perceptions of the organization's commitment to the service relationship.* • *Allow organizations to measure how perceptions change over time.*	• *Too many surveys lead to fatigue, and scores which do not reflect actual opinions.* • *Follow-ups may be seen as an attempt to sell more rather than to understand better; they may be ignored.* • *Responses may be strongly influenced by when customers and users are solicited.*

---

[11] *ITIL® 4: Direct, Plan and Improve*, table 3.12. Copyright © AXELOS Limited 2020.

4: Focus on improvement

> Your customers and users will engage with you in good faith if they believe you will take positive action based on their responses. If customers and users don't think you will take any action, then they won't spend time giving you their views. It's important to be transparent about the actions taken (or not) as a result of customer/user satisfaction analysis.

Assessment method 5 – SLA achievement analysis

An SLA is *"a documented agreement between a service provider and a customer that identifies both the services required and the expected level of service"*.

An improvement initiative may be triggered by the failure to meet SLA targets. SLA achievement analysis is an example of ongoing assessment linked to service quality.

The following table outlines some of the pros and cons of SLA analysis:

4: Focus on improvement

Table 9: Pros and Cons of SLA Achievement Analyses[12]

Pros	Cons
• *Information about SLA achievements initiates productive conversations about the performance, priorities, and future of service relationships.* • *SLA achievement motivates continued achievement, as both the provider and consumer realize its value.* • *Metrics used for SLA achievement assessment are among the best understood metrics, making them an excellent source of ideas for improvements.*	• *If the targets established in an SLA do not reflect what service consumers want and need, the assessment of whether or not they have been achieved will not reflect the consumers' satisfaction.* • *The underlying causes of issues with SLA achievement may be difficult to discover and complex to solve.*

---

[12] *ITIL® 4: Direct, Plan and Improve*, table 3.13. Copyright © AXELOS Limited 2020.

4: Focus on improvement

Assessment method 6 – benchmarking

"Benchmarking is the act of measuring the performance of an organization's products, services, or practices against those of a similar organization. Comparing an organization to one that performs better may highlight change initiatives that could yield tangible improvements. Benchmarking should be a regular exercise as part of the continual improvement practice, allowing organizations to match or surpass their competitors' performances.

It is also a valuable tool for motivating cultural change based on the premise that organizations can become the standard that other organizations measure themselves against. Although benchmarking is generally done at an organizational level, it can be valuable to compare specific areas of high-performing organizations. For example, a problem manager may want to understand what another organization with a lower major incident occurrence rate does differently in its problem management practice. Talking to counterparts in similar roles can provide valuable insights, which may lead to worthy improvement initiatives.

Before enacting a benchmark comparison, it is important to ensure that the organizations being compared are truly comparable. Two organizations in the same industry, for example, may serve significantly different markets, making a benchmark comparison less relevant and less valuable."

The following table outlines the pros and cons of benchmarking:

4: Focus on improvement

Table 10: Pros and Cons of Benchmarking[13]

Pros	Cons
• Places a focus on ideas for improvement. • Provides quantitative and explicit standards for organizations to compare themselves against. • Provides a means for competitive analysis or potential partnering. • Can examine against multiple industries.	• Does not always transfer well between organizations without context. • Does not measure effectiveness. • Can introduce industry bias based on revenue rather than practice. • Aims to identify industry leaders, leading to standardized, but not necessarily ideal, behaviours.

Assessment method 7 – Maturity assessments

Maturity assessments compare a capability with a framework, model or scale. The results are presented as a rating or level, which allows the organisation to see if it needs to make any improvements.

Table 11 outlines some of the pros and cons of maturity assessments:

---

[13] *ITIL® 4: Direct, Plan and Improve*, table 3.14. Copyright © AXELOS Limited 2020.

4: Focus on improvement

Table 11: Pros and Cons of Maturity Assessments[14]

Pros	Cons
• *Facilitate the prioritization of resources to effect maturity. Provide a baseline for measuring improvement.* • *Set specific maturity targets, thereby giving organizations a focus for their efforts.*	• *Different perspectives of maturity may impede an organization's ability to progress.* • *Can be costly for organizations or processes to mature.* • *There is a risk of aiming to move up the maturity levels rather than improving the organization or its processes.*

Using assessments

Many organisations use a variety of assessment methods. It's important to apply the right ones at the right time, and make sure the scope and objectives are clearly understood.

The role and scope of each assessment type need to be defined. If the assessment is too broad, it can be expensive and time-consuming, with unclear results. If the scope is too narrow, there may not be enough information to support decision-making. The assessment objective needs to be

---

[14] *ITIL® 4: Direct, Plan and Improve*, table 3.15. Copyright © AXELOS Limited 2020.

4: Focus on improvement

clearly defined. This can be done by asking questions such as:

- *"What are the assessment's objectives?*
  - *What information is needed from the assessment?*
  - *Who is the audience for the assessment report?*
- *What is needed to be able to perform the assessment?*
  - *Who will conduct the assessment?*
  - *Who needs to participate in the assessment?*
  - *Which areas of the organization or SVS will be in the assessment's scope?*
  - *What materials or technologies are needed for the assessment?*
- *What criteria will be used for the assessment?*
  - *What will the assessment's definition of success be?*
  - *What specific aspects of the in-scope parts of the organization or SVS must be examined?*
- *What outputs are expected from the assessment?*
  - *What form should the assessment output take?*
  - *What metrics need to be included in the assessment output?*
  - *What questions should the assessment answer?"*

If the assessment is used as part of an ongoing discovery or improvement programme, these questions will need to be revisited regularly to make sure the answers are still relevant.

4: Focus on improvement

> There are external organisations that specialise in carrying out assessments. Using their expertise can be extremely valuable throughout the full lifecycle of an assessment. Everything from scoping to designing questions (where appropriate) can be made easier with some specialist support. If the assessment includes looking at people's roles and how work is carried out, you may find you get more honest responses if the assessor is perceived as neutral by the responder.

Building a business case

A business case provides *"justification for the expenditure of organizational resources, providing information about costs, benefits, options, risks, and issues"*.

Business cases are used to support improvement initiatives, as well as in many other business contexts. As part of an improvement initiative, you will need to be able to build a business case, communicate its key points and advocate to win support for your plans.

Each organisation will define the circumstances that require a business case, often based on a threshold of financial investment. Business cases act as decision support and planning tools, allowing effective investment decisions to be made. The core elements of a business case are:

- Proposal;

4: Focus on improvement

- Benefits;
- Risks; and
- Investment justification.

Some organisations will use the same template for all business cases, and others will use a scale depending on the size of investment required. Financial analysis is a critical part of the business case, and again, many organisations will have detailed guidance and templates already in place. The portfolio management practice can provide support and guidance about portfolio investment prioritisation. The business case must show that the product or service will add value, lead to improvement or avoid a negative consequence.

To build a successful business case, consider using workshops and including stakeholders and senior managers. These workshops can address questions including:

- *"What problems are we looking to solve?*
- *What will be the scope of the product/service?*
- *Who will be its consumers?*
- *What outcomes or added value are we expecting?*
- *How will we measure success?"*

Organisational conditions and constraints will affect what is possible for any change or improvement. These elements must be factored in, or there is a risk the business case will be unrealistic. Table 12 shows some examples:

4: Focus on improvement

Table 12: Examples of Organisational Conditions and Constraints

Pace of change	• How much change can the organisation manage in a specific period? • Does it have a history of successful changes? • What other initiatives are happening at the same time?
Culture	• Does the organisational culture facilitate or inhibit change? • Are there consistent practices in place?
Resource availability and capacity	• Does the change require new or existing resources? • Are existing resources already at full capacity? • What funding is available for extra resources?
Budget restrictions	• Are there any spending freezes or restrictions in place? • When do budget requests need to be submitted? • Are there other funding requests with a higher priority?

4: Focus on improvement

> I've found that many organisations use business case templates that have evolved over time from a relatively simple document to something more unwieldy. Apply the ITIL principles to your business case template and ask yourself "what are we actually trying to achieve?". The principles 'keep it simple and practical' and 'focus on value' are important guidelines here. If there are sections in the template that are there purely to tick a box, get rid of them. If your document is short and to the point (an executive summary business case almost), your reviewers are more likely to read it in full and absorb what's important.

Communicating and advocating for a business case

Business cases that do not align with the organisation's overall vision and objectives are likely to be rejected. Each business case will be assessed via an approval process, often involving senior managers.

The business case author or change agent will need to prepare their business case carefully. This includes using the right language, tone and format, and perhaps involving some of the potential approvers in the creation of the business case, so there are no surprises later in the process.

Before the business case is formally reviewed, the author or change agent should:

4: Focus on improvement

- Speak with stakeholders and understand their priorities;
- Review organisational objectives;
- Check existing business cases and portfolios for potential conflicts; and
- Try to anticipate any possible objections.

The business case may be presented, with a question and answer session to discuss any queries or objections. The author or change agent will need to prepare carefully for a presentation, including practice sessions and trying to anticipate questions.

> Think about how business is actually done in your country, your culture and your organisation. In some countries, it's a really good idea to talk to the people who will sign off your business case before it's formally assessed and doing so will increase your chance of a successful result. In a different culture, this could be seen as highly inappropriate. We all need to work within the constraints of our environment, and tailor guidance to our own situation.

Improvement reviews

An improvement review is an *"evaluation using metrics and other evidence to determine whether an improvement has achieved its desired outcomes and, if not, what needs to be*

4: Focus on improvement

done to complete the work". It is sometimes referred to as a benefits realisation review.

Improvement reviews relate to step 6 of the continual improvement model – Did we get there? A review checks the progress and value delivered by an iteration of an improvement initiative. These checks need to be based on factual information, using metrics to validate success or highlight any gaps.

Objective review data comes from key performance indicators (KPIs – a quantifiable measure used to evaluate the success of an organisation, employee, etc. in meeting objectives for performance), agreed success factors and other metrics. Subjective evidence including opinion surveys and stakeholders reports and feedback can also be inputs to the review. If benefits haven't been delivered, the plan will need to be revisited and possibly updated (or even abandoned).

The amount of time and effort spent on the review work will be dictated by the complexity and size of the improvement project. A review might be very formal and structured, or informal and unstructured. Most improvement plans include activities to measure progress and confirm if value has been delivered. Sometimes, there are unexpected results or additional lessons are learned. Capturing these during a review will ensure they become inputs for future improvement projects.

Analysis of lessons learned

Lessons learned relate mainly to step 7 of the continual improvement model – How do we keep momentum going?

At the end of this step, change agents should have:

- Confirmed the improvements are established;

4: Focus on improvement

- A list of recommendations for further improvement initiatives or iterations; and
- A documented lessons-learned analysis.

When an improvement initiative is in progress, change agents need to manage it carefully to avoid scope creep. 'Scope creep' is a term that originated in project management. Also referred to as 'requirement creep', it refers to changes or continuous or uncontrolled growth in a project's scope. This can occur when the scope of a project is not properly defined, documented or controlled. New improvement ideas that are suggested during the improvement initiative need to be recorded so they can be considered in the future. This allows them to be managed without automatically adding them to the scope of the existing initiative. This is often done via a continual improvement register.

Lessons-learned analysis is the *"evaluation of an improvement initiative or iteration for the purpose of understanding what did or did not go well and what should be done differently in the future in similar circumstances"*.

Where are lessons learned captured in your organisation? Is there enough time to capture them and apply them?

The way that lessons learned are captured and applied is one area where I've seen some quite significant

> differences with organisations working in an Agile or a waterfall way.
>
> In an Agile environment, review time is often built into the development calendar. This leads to reviews being taken seriously with time allocated to them, improving the quality of lessons learned. Agile teams often stay with their product from development through to operation, so knowledge stays within the team. In a waterfall project, any slippage in the timetable can lead to less time being available for reviews and lessons learned. Staff might be reallocated at the end of the project, so the knowledge they have is spread throughout the organisation. This can be a benefit if their lessons learned relate to how they work, but a risk if their knowledge is related to a specific product or service.

Analysis of the continual improvement practice will show what activities went well (or didn't), and how these lessons can be applied to future improvement activities. Lessons need to be documented all the way through an improvement initiative, whenever they arise. Lessons learned should be captured in a log throughout the improvement initiative. At the end of the initiative, this log is reviewed and is an input for the lessons learned report. These reports are then used as an input to future improvement initiatives. Without learning from these lessons, future improvements are more likely to fail, and it can be more challenging to embed an improvement culture. The primary focus should always be on learning, not blame.

4: Focus on improvement

Embedding an improvement culture

Senior management backing is essential to support an improvement culture. Managers need to embed continual improvement values and support the continual improvement practice. A culture of continual improvement:

- *"Encourages stakeholders to suggest and support improvements*
- *Encourages stakeholders to express their needs, wants, and concerns and to take risks*
- *Recognizes that perfectionism is typically self-defeating and blocks timely improvements*
- *Considers continual improvement to be a business as usual (BAU) activity*
- *Celebrates successful improvements*
- *Encourages fast feedback loops*
- *Promotes learning from failures rather than a blame culture."*

> When it comes to improvement, the most important thing to do is start! Start small if necessary, within your own sphere of control, to deliver results that will build momentum. What could you do during your next day at work? Is there something that's been annoying you?

CHAPTER 5: FOCUS ON ORGANISATIONAL CHANGE MANAGEMENT

Organisational change management (OCM) enables many direction, planning and improvement activities. The DPI syllabus requires you to understand topics including:

- The nature, scope, and potential benefits of OCM;
- Using OCM key principles and methods to:
  - Identify and manage different types of stakeholders;
  - Effectively communicate with and influence others;
  - Establish effective feedback channels; and
  - Establish effective interfaces across the service value chain.

> Take a moment to think about any significant changes you have been affected by, for example a merger or acquisition, an office move, or organisation rebrand. How did you feel? Did you have all the information you needed? What did the organisation's OCM practice do well, and what could it have done better?

The nature of OCM

OCM provides a structured approach to allow improvements to take place smoothly and successfully. It deals with the

5: Focus on organisational change management

human side of change, to support long-lasting benefits. Every change or improvement has an impact on people. It can affect their:

- Work;
- Behaviour; and
- Roles.

Every improvement initiative relies on these five elements:

- Clear and relevant objectives.
- Strong, committed leadership.
- Willing, prepared participants.
- Demonstrated value.
- Sustained improvement.

Table 13 shows more information about these elements.

Table 13: Five Elements for a Successful Improvement Initiative[15]

Requirement	*Details*	*How OCM helps*
Clear and relevant objectives	To gain maximum support, improvements require objectives that are clear enough for people to	Improvement objectives must be communicated to stakeholders, who should then discuss them. If adjustments are made, their

---

[15] *ITIL® 4: Direct, Plan and Improve*, table 6.3. Copyright © AXELOS Limited 2020.

5: Focus on organisational change management

	understand and which make sense relative to the target organization.	nature and the reasons for them must also be communicated.
Strong and committed leadership	It is critical that improvements are actively supported by leaders within the organization. If their commitments are visible, overall buy-in is likely to increase.	Each sponsor and leader should be identified, and their roles and responsibilities communicated to the initiative's stakeholders.
Willing and prepared participants	People may resist a change for a variety of reasons. However, improvements need participants who are willing to change. People are often more willing to	OCM allows for resistance to be identified, understood, and overcome using a resistance management plan. OCM uses a training plan to ensure that people have the skills and knowledge to

5: Focus on organisational change management

	change when they feel they are suitably prepared.	change successfully, and a communication plan to manage change updates.
Demonstrated value	To keep the change moving forward, stakeholders must be convinced of its value before it is achieved, and able to recognize the value after it has been achieved.	OCM runs communication programmes to share any expected and achieved benefits with stakeholders, solidifying their commitment to the current effort and willingness to support future similar efforts.
Sustained improvement	Many improvements fail when people revert to old ways of working. Even when an individual improvement succeeds, organizations can fail to	The OCM practice seeks to continually reinforce the value of the change through regular communication and the support of

5: Focus on organisational change management

	sustain the momentum with more improvement.	*sponsors and leaders.*

OCM and DPI

Direction, planning and improvement activities all rely on OCM. The human element has to be considered for every activity in DPI.

Table 14: OCM and DPI

OCM and Direction	When an organisation maps and communicates its vision and mission, it uses these to direct and drive behaviour. OCM helps to increase the likelihood of direction being successful. If an organisation wants to change how its employees act, OCM principles and methods can help accomplish this.
OCM and Planning	Planning activities need to integrate OCM activities. OCM isn't something that can be added in at the end,

5: Focus on organisational change management

	and we can't assume it will 'just happen'. OCM can be applied to plans at all levels: strategic, tactical and operational.
OCM and Improvement	OCM also supports improvement. It can help build commitment and encourage participation, increasing the chance of an improvement being successful. The OCM practice is involved in improvement in these ways: *"It ensures that the people involved in implementing improvement initiatives do so effectively and efficiently.* *It ensures that the people impacted by changes resulting from improvement initiatives accept and adopt those changes"*

5: Focus on organisational change management

The purpose of OCM

The purpose of the OCM practice is *"to ensure that changes in an organization are implemented smoothly and successfully, and that lasting benefits are achieved by managing the human aspects of the changes"*.

> OCM doesn't exist as a separate function in most of the organisations I've worked with. When a large project or programme launches, OCM is treated as a workstream within the overall project or programme. This isn't necessarily a bad thing, but unless an organisation has very effective knowledge management, where does OCM knowledge reside? How does the OCM workstream in a programme learn from past lessons?
>
> Most organisations now recognise they are living in a 'VUCA' world – volatile, uncertain, complex and ambiguous. Change is constant and ongoing, not an event that happens every 12–18 months. How do we adapt our OCM practices to meet the demands of the world we live in? OCM needs to become an organisational muscle that we can flex when we need to; it's something we need to train constantly so that it improves all the time. That doesn't necessarily imply an OCM 'team', but it does suggest that organisations need to think carefully about where their OCM capabilities are and how they are integrated into different roles.

5: Focus on organisational change management

OCM supports and enables organisational growth, improvement and evolution. The people element of any organisational change is critical. The OCM practice supports successful organisational change by creating a value-driven environment across the organisation. It needs to understand who the stakeholders for a change are, and their expectations and values. People's response to changes and their ability to adopt new behaviour can dictate the success or failure of a change.

OCM contributes to every part of the service value system, following these three premises:

- It is integrated into value streams to ensure changes are effective, safe and aligned with stakeholder expectations.
- It does not try to unify all changes into one big picture; this is not necessary or possible.
- It is focused on balancing effectiveness, agility, compliance and risk control for all changes in its scope.

OCM key terms and concepts

Three important concepts for OCM are change, transformation and evolution.

"**Change** is a different way of executing tasks. Doing it as it has previously been done, but in a more efficient and productive way. Change uses external impact to modify actions."

"**Transformation** is a different way of working. It involves changes in beliefs, values, and wishes. Transformation results shift in the organizational system and as a result, in

5: Focus on organisational change management

personal and organizational behavior. The transformation is based on learning from previous mistakes."

*"**Evolution** is a state of continual improvement through transformation and change. The foundation of evolution is constant adjustments in values, beliefs, and behavior, with the use of internal and external feedback."*

Change and transformation mean different things. Change agents or stakeholders need to understand if they are executing a change or a transformation, in order to apply the right methods and achieve the desired results. A series of changes may contribute to an organisation's overall transformation.

> The biggest change affecting many organisations today is digital transformation. Digital transformation is on the agenda at the highest levels, but many organisations have a fuzzy understanding of what it actually is and what it means for their organisation. Digital teams are created and new roles (e.g. Chief Digital Officer) are assigned, but outcomes aren't clearly defined. This can lead to a lot of wasted time and effort.
>
> If digital transformation is on your organisation's agenda, think about what the term means to the stakeholders in your organisation. Will your organisation actually be transformed, with the level of change that implies, or is your focus on digital optimisation, making improvements

5: Focus on organisational change management

> to how work is carried out by using technology? Once you understand the nature and scope of a change, you can begin to plan to deliver it successfully.

Emotional, social and system intelligence

Organisational changes can be complex situations. Stakeholders who wish to make a change need to demonstrate presence, consciousness, self-leadership and responsibility. They must focus on individuals, relationships between them, and systems in general. To create flexible, resilient and fulfilled individuals, teams and systems, organisations need to develop three forms of intelligence.

*"**Emotional Intelligence** is the ability to access, express, and use one's emotions in an efficient way. It describes having emotional self-awareness and the capacity to manage feelings by directing them toward goals. It also ensures the ability to self-motivate, suppress impulsive actions, and delay immediate satisfaction in order to achieve the goals."*

*"**Social intelligence** builds on emotional intelligence. It is the capability to identify emotions of other people by not making assumptions, being empathetic, and open to co-creative actions and new ways of working in order to achieve common goals and build positive relationships. It also includes knowing and using social roles and rules, effective listening, and conversational skills."*

5: Focus on organisational change management

Emotional and social intelligence build 'soft skills', the human side of our roles in IT and service management. They're easy to gloss over, easy to underestimate and very, very challenging to recruit for. Once you recognise you need these skills in your organisation, you will likely need to make changes to help your people develop them. This includes recruiting the right people, creating role descriptions that value soft skills, and providing training and development opportunities.

One example of how these skills are underrated is how managers are appointed. Many organisations I work with move people into management roles based on length of service, or experience with a product. Someone who has been a very happy engineer for five years is suddenly thrust into a management role, and the organisation assumes they will know how to cope (or even that they want the role in the first place!).

*"**Systems intelligence** is the ability to understand, reflect upon, express, and incorporate the wider context of the system(s) a human interacts within into actions. It combines sensitivity about the environment with system thinking. In regard to the ITIL guiding principles, it is based on the ability to think and work holistically, while focusing on value, in the context of adaptive complex systems. It is the capability to see oneself as a part of a system, identify system*

5: Focus on organisational change management

characteristics, be aware of system rules and patterns, and be able to contribute to a system development consciously."

Values-based organisational change

Values reflect people's principles, ideas and beliefs. If an organisation's culture reflects its employees' values, it is likely to get good results from its staff and experience less resistance to change.

Organisational culture is based on shared values. OCM needs to have an understanding of the organisation's values and how they relate to individual values and the desired outcome of any change.

> ❓
>
> What values does your organisation have? Are values clearly articulated, for example are they clearly displayed in the workplace? Do your organisation's stated values match its actual culture as you experience it? For example, if an organisation talks about learning lessons rather than apportioning blame, does that reflect what really happens when something goes wrong?

Figure 7[16] shows value-based organisational change.

---

[16] *Organizational change management – ITIL® 4 Practice Guide*, figure 2.1. Copyright © AXELOS Limited 2020.

5: Focus on organisational change management

Level	Name	Description
7	Service	**Service to the humanity and the planet** — Social responsibility, future generations, long-term perspective, ethics, compassion, humanity.
6	Making a difference	**Strategic partnerships and alliances** — Environmental awareness, community involvement, employee fulfilment, coaching/mentoring.
5	Internal cohesion	**Building internal community** — Shared vision and values, commitment, integrity, trust, passion, creativity, openness, transparency.
4	Transformation	**Continuous renewal and learning** — Accountability, adaptability, empowerment, teamwork, goals orientation, personal growth.
3	Self-esteem	**High performance** — Systems, processes, quality, best practices, pride in performance. Bureaucracy, complacency.
2	Relationship	**Harmonious relationships** — Loyalty, open communication, customer satisfaction, friendship. Manipulation, blame.
1	Survival	**Financial stability** — Shareholder value, organisational growth, employee health, safety. Control, corruption, greed.

Figure 7: Value based organisational change

5: Focus on organisational change management

Organisations that focus exclusively on the satisfaction of the lower needs are not adaptable and do not empower employees. Consequently, there is little enthusiasm within the workforce, and there is little innovation and creativity. These organisations are often ruled by fear and are not healthy places to work. Employees often feel frustrated and complain about stress. Organisational changes are usually not successful in this type of organisation.

Organisations that focus exclusively on the satisfaction of the higher needs lack the basic business skills and capabilities necessary to operate effectively. They are ineffectual and impractical when it comes to financial matters. They are not customer oriented, and they lack the systems and processes necessary for high performance.

The most successful organisations are those that have mastered both their "deficiency" needs and their "growth" needs. They create a climate of trust, have the ability to manage complexity and can respond or rapidly adapt to all situations. These organisations present environments for transformation and evolution.

Organisational change principles

Each organisation will define its own management, leadership and motivation approach for OCM. Practices are continually evolving, and the OCM practice will adopt different approaches depending on the level of complexity related to the change. Table 15 shows some examples of principles to guide organisational change:

5: Focus on organisational change management

Table 15: Principles to Guide Organisational Change

Clear and relevant objectives	The change objectives must be based on the organisation's vision and values and be clearly communicated to all stakeholders. The change must deliver real value.
Strong and committed leadership	The OCM practice should create an environment where people can participate in leadership as a shared practice. Anyone can contribute to or lead a change initiative, drawing on leadership capabilities from across the organisation. Leadership should be flexible and open, not fixed.
Willing and prepared participants	Organisations need to focus on encouraging and supporting human capital, not forcing through changes, and overcoming resistance. The OCM practice needs to have a human-centred design, recognising that stakeholders can be

5: Focus on organisational change management

	valuable change agents. Changes should be based on intrinsic motivation, not extrinsic reinforcement.
Sustained improvement	OCM should focus on co-created change, to maintain focus and bring multiple stakeholder groups together. Systems should continually evolve to support organisational change results.

Think about the My Way project at Banksbest. Does it have:

- Clear and relevant objectives?
- Strong and committed leadership?
- Willing and prepared participants?

The scope of OCM

The scope of the OCM practice includes:

5: Focus on organisational change management

- *"Designing, implementing, and continually improving an adaptive approach for a developing environment in an organization*
- *Planning and improving organizational change approaches and methods*
- *Scheduling and coordinating all ongoing changes through the whole lifecycle*
- *Communicating change plans and progress to relevant stakeholders*
- *Assessing change success, including outputs, outcomes, efficiency, risks, and costs."*

Tables 16 and 17 show more detail about the OCM practice.

Table 16: Organizational Changes in the Four Dimensions of Service Management[17]

Dimension of service management	Areas subject to potential organizational change	Scoping considerations
Information and technology	• Hardware and software • Service architecture • Service design	Usually addressed by the change enablement practice in conjunction with

---

[17] *ITIL® 4: Direct, Plan and Improve*, table 2.1. Copyright © AXELOS Limited 2020.

5: Focus on organisational change management

	• Technical and user documentation	the project management, service design, and architecture management practices. Some OCM activities may be used to support training, design, and so on
Organizations and people	• Organizational structure • Roles and responsibilities • Culture and rules of work behaviour • Personal competencies	Usually addressed by the OCM in conjunction with the project management, workforce and talent management, and relationship management practices
Value streams and processes	• Value streams architecture • Work processes and procedures	May be addressed by the change enablement together with the OCM

5: Focus on organisational change management

	• Process documentation	practice and/or other practices
Partners and suppliers	• Service dependencies on third parties at the architecture level • Contractual arrangements with third parties (new suppliers, change of responsibilities, and so on.) • Contract and other documents (version changes, prolongation, and so on.)	May be addressed by the change enablement practice in conjunction with the supplier management, OCM and/or other practices

5: Focus on organisational change management

Table 17: Activities Related to the OCM Practice that are Described in other Practice Guides[18]

Activity	Practice guide
Organizational change initiation	All other practices
Organizational change plan and adaptive environment design and realization	Relationship management Workforce and talent management Strategy management Continual improvement
Change of IT infrastructure related to the organizational change	Change enablement Release management Business analysis Deployment management Software development and management Service validation and testing Portfolio management Service catalogue management

---

[18] *ITIL® 4: Direct, Plan and Improve*, table 2.2. Copyright © AXELOS Limited 2020.

5: Focus on organisational change management

Change risks assessment and control	Risk management
Costs control, financial evaluation of changes	Service financial management
Management of projects	Project management
Definition of vision and strategic objectives	Strategy management
Continual improvement in all four dimensions of service management	Continual improvement

OCM practice success factors

A practice success factor (PSF) is *"a complex functional component of a practice that is required for the practice to fulfil its purpose"*. PSFs include elements from all four dimensions of service management.

The OCM practice has three PSFs:

- *"Creating and maintaining a change-enabling culture across the organization*
- *Establishing and maintaining a holistic approach and continual improvement for organizational change management*
- *Ensuring organizational changes are realized in an effective manner, leading to stakeholders' satisfaction and meeting compliance requirements."*

5: Focus on organisational change management

Viewing OCM as a practice, rather than treating it as a series of siloed workstreams attached to projects and programmes, allows it to be measured for effectiveness. This will highlight opportunities for improvement and identify if the practice is misaligned with the organisation's overall vision and goals. You can see the clear links to effective DPI in this type of scenario.

Table 18: The OCM Practice Success Factors

"Creating and maintaining a change-enabling culture across the organization"	A change-enabling culture allows people within an organisation to share these elements related to changes: • Beliefs • Attitudes • Values • Common knowledge • Expectations OCM can only be effective with commitment from stakeholders. This is supported by a culture that encourages people to speak up, challenge things, and to

5: Focus on organisational change management

	listen and communicate effectively. A change-enabling culture will affect internal communication, but it may also extend to relationships with suppliers and partners.
	These practices support OCM for this PSF:
	• Workforce and talent management. • Relationship management. • Strategy management. • Continual improvement management.
"Establishing and maintaining a holistic approach and continual improvement for organizational change management"	Like any practice, OCM should be continually improved. Improvements affect changes themselves, principles, methods, processes, tools and other resources.
	Once improvements are identified, they should be tracked and implemented, using guidance from the continual improvement practice. All practices, including OCM, also

5: Focus on organisational change management

	contribute to value streams and support the continual improvement of services.
"Ensuring organizational changes are realized in an effective manner, leading to stakeholders' satisfaction and meeting compliance requirements"	OCM has to understand who its stakeholders are, and their level of interest and involvement. Stakeholders can include, among others: • Service provider teams; • Users; • Customers; • Service provision sponsors; • Service consumption sponsors; and • Suppliers and partners. The OCM practice will identify stakeholders and should understand their values and expectations. The practice will work with relationship management, business analysis and risk management in this area. Stakeholder engagement and satisfaction needs to be captured before, during and after a change, and any corrective action or

5: Focus on organisational change management

	improvement taken where necessary. This will include using techniques like status updates and feedback collection.
	OCM is often affected by governance and compliance requirements. The practice will support these areas by: • Including any necessary controls in plans, processes and procedures; • Providing any necessary reports or information; and • Initiating improvements to prevent or correct any non-compliance.

Key metrics

A practice can only be measured within the context of its application. In other words, within the value streams it supports. Key metrics for OCM can be mapped to its PSFs and used as KPIs in the context of value streams. Table 19 shows some examples of key OCM metrics:

5: Focus on organisational change management

Table 19: Key Metrics for the OCM Practice[19]

Practice success factors	*Key metrics*
Creating and maintaining a change-enabling culture across the organization	• *Awareness of the organizational change, principles, and methods across the organization* • *Attitude towards organizational changes across the organization* • *Level of resistance to changes* • *Alignment in attitude to changes at different levels of the organization*
Establishing and maintaining a holistic approach and continual improvement for organizational change management	• *Stakeholder satisfaction with the procedures and communications* • *Amount of improvements initiated by the OCM practice* • *Stakeholders satisfaction with knowledge about up to*

---

[19] *ITIL® 4: Direct, Plan and Improve*, table 2.3. Copyright © AXELOS Limited 2020.

5: Focus on organisational change management

	date transformational methods and tools
Ensuring organizational changes are realized in an effective manner, leading to stakeholders' satisfaction and meeting compliance requirements	• *Change initiators' satisfaction with change outcomes* • *Change success/acceptance rate over period* • *Compliance with formally stated requirements, according to audit reports* • *Change initiators' satisfaction with change timeliness* • *Stakeholder satisfaction with realization of individual changes*

?

Do any of these key metrics currently exist in your organisation? Where would you start to measure the effectiveness of OCM in your organisation?

The Banksbest case study mentions that the organisation's rebrand has confused some of its customers and the digital transformation programme hasn't delivered many results

5: Focus on organisational change management

> yet. Could better OCM capabilities have improved the situation?

OCM and communication

The DPI syllabus looks at the relationship between OCM and communication, including how to:

- Identify and communicate with stakeholders;
- Map stakeholders;
- Develop a stakeholder communication plan;
- Understand the basics of effective communication;
- Use different communication methods and media; and
- Define and establish feedback channels.

Stakeholder identification and management

"A stakeholder is a person or organization that has an interest or involvement in an organization, product, service, practice, or other entity."

Stakeholders can include:

- Customers
- Users
- Sponsors
- Suppliers
- Shareholders
- Partners

For each stakeholder, it is important to identify:

- What interest do they have in the outcome of the work? Positive or negative?

5: Focus on organisational change management

- What is their primary motivation? What information do they need?
- How do they want to receive information?
- What is their current opinion of the initiative? Is it based on good information?
- Who influences their opinions? Are some of these influencers important stakeholders in their own right?
- What will win them round to support the improvement?
- If it is doubtful they can be won over, how can their opposition be managed?
- Who might be influenced by their opinions?

Stakeholders can be categorised using a matrix to map high or low power/influence/impact and high or low interest/involvement.

- **Major stakeholders**
  - Have high power/influence/impact but low interest/involvement.
  - This type of stakeholder needs to be kept satisfied.
- **Critical stakeholders**
  - Have high power/influence/impact and high interest/involvement.
  - This type of stakeholder needs to be fully engaged.
- **Minor stakeholders**
  - Have low power/influence/impact and low interest/involvement.
  - This type of stakeholder needs to be monitored and informed.
- **Significant stakeholders**

5: Focus on organisational change management

- Have low power/influence/impact and high interest/involvement.
- This type of stakeholder needs to be kept adequately informed and engaged.

Remember that stakeholder classifications can change, so they need to be regularly reassessed.

The level of effort and formality that can be applied to stakeholder management seems excessive to many organisations, particularly when they see their project or change as being 'fairly small' or one that 'no one will really notice'.

I would suggest that getting to know your stakeholders and building strong relationships with them is one of the single most important things you can do if you are involved with any type of product or service. When organisations don't know their stakeholders, so many decisions are made based on assumptions. This can lead to huge amounts of wasted time and effort. Stakeholder management is an ongoing relationship that needs to be nurtured and will deliver more and more benefits over time. The confusion around the rebrand at Banksbest, for example, could have been avoided with better communication and stakeholder management. If you've got access to it, it's worth reading the ITIL 4 relationship management practice. Also take a look at the work of the BRM Institute (*www.brm.institute*)

5: Focus on organisational change management

> for more good practice related to value creation and stakeholder management.

Stakeholder communication

Effective communication is an essential component of OCM. Communication needs to happen all the way through a change, to communicate the essential information – what, why, when, how and where?

Communication can take a significant amount of time, so it needs to be planned carefully. Groups or user personas can be used to manage targeted communication (a persona is a realistic but fictional character built to represent a type of user who has common requirements for a site, brand or product). Influential stakeholders may require personal communication; communication should be tailored to ensure their continuing support. Communication should endeavour to reduce resistance, although it may not be possible to overcome it completely.

> Think about how brands communicate with you. Which brands do it well? Which brands annoy you?
>
> What about internal communication in the organisation you work for? Is that effective?

Communication should be automated where appropriate, but remember to focus on 'intelligent' communication and don't

5: Focus on organisational change management

frustrate the people you interact with. Effective communication should be considered as:

- A key business skill;
- Fundamental to service management, projects, processes, improvements, etc.;
- More than being 'nice' (but that helps);
- Being efficient, responsive, professional and effective; and
- A way to recognise the intellectual and emotional needs of other people.

Communication principles include:

- Communication is a two-way process;
- We are all communicating all the time;
- Timing and frequency matters;
- There is no single method of communication that works for everyone; and
- The message is in the medium.

Here are some communication tips:

- There is no single method of communication that works for everyone – we all have preferences.
- Know who you're communicating with and choose how to communicate – consider alternative options, for both message and format.
- Good timing is essential – understand business periods when there is high activity and priority.
- Send customer satisfaction surveys after major initiatives/incidents.

5: Focus on organisational change management

- Don't over- or under-communicate.
- Get close to your customers and stakeholders and form a relationship.

Communication is a two-way process

When you communicate something, you cannot assume the message has been understood. The communicator is responsible for checking that the message was received and any actions are underway. The message receiver also needs to confirm their understanding of the message is correct.

Formal and informal checks and tests should be used to make sure messages are being understood. Communication is a skill that develops over time, and people are more likely to engage in communication and collaboration if they feel they are being listened to.

> You know from the case study that the rebrand at Banksbest led to some confusion among customers. What communication plan would you have recommended?

Some communication is delivered non-verbally, through body language, or tone of voice. These cues can have more impact than the words that are being said. Good communicators use high emotional intelligence to interpret their listener's reactions and adapt their communication accordingly. Project managers and change agents will use a

5: Focus on organisational change management

portfolio of communication techniques to get the results they need.

No single method of communication works for everyone. Using a range of techniques will help get the message across. Tailor the messages to the expected audience and try to check whether the message has been received and understood.

A lot of communication best practice focuses on body language, non-verbal cues, etc. This assumes that communication is face-to-face, whereas many of us now have to communicate via email, videoconferencing and conference calls. This creates new challenges, and you may have experienced (as I have) how a poorly worded email can create offence or lead to key information being missed.

Consider whether you need guidance and training in your organisation to help people communicate effectively across all channels. This could include simple guidance (for example: don't use 'u' instead of 'you' in written communication in an organisation with a formal culture) as well as broader principles to help your colleagues look after themselves (for example: don't assume you can go straight from one virtual meeting to another because there is no travel time to account for – make sure you give yourself the chance to pause and absorb before you move on).

5: Focus on organisational change management

The message is the medium

The format of a message can affect whether it is received and understood. For example, putting video into an email might mean it is marked as 'junk' and never seen. Choose the format, style, size and medium for each message carefully. Formal content may require a more formal medium.

> One of my earliest roles was managing customer service for a retail organisation that had just introduced its first websites. Communicating via email was seen as a huge novelty, and most customers preferred to follow up with a phone call as they didn't trust that emails would be received or processed. Compare that to the way many of us shop and interact with brands now. We are accustomed to using email and even social media to chat with brands; getting a phone call would seem unusual and a letter even more so. But there's a time and a place for everything, and it's important to choose the right medium at the right time.

Communication methods and media

There are many different communication methods. They can be:

- Direct or indirect (remote);
- Real-time or delayed; and
- One-directional or interactive.

5: Focus on organisational change management

Table 20 shows more information.

Table 20: Examples of Communication Methods[20]

Method	Details	Contact	Timing	Inter-action
One on one/face to face	One-on-one interactions are the best way to have good interactions and build relationships. They should always be considered when resolving issues. The development of immersive ambient videoconf-erencing, along with some simple collaboration tools, has also improved the	Direct	Real-time	High

---

[20] *ITIL® 4: Direct, Plan and Improve*, table 6.1. Copyright © AXELOS Limited 2020.

5: Focus on organisational change management

	experience of and opportunities for digital face-to-face interactions.			
Meetings/ workshops	Meetings and workshops are essential tools for progressing projects. All good communicators should know how to run meetings effectively. A meeting's quality and delivery can be a useful gauge of an organization's culture, showing whether it demonstrates professionalism and competence.	Direct	Real-time	High
Telephone	Like a physical conversation, telephone	Direct	Real-time	High

5: Focus on organisational change management

	communication can dissect issues and accelerate the exchange of information. It is possible to infer certain aspects of a person's emotional state while using a telephone, through their tone of voice, volume, and language choices.			

Defining and establishing feedback channels

Monitoring feedback helps identify whether messages are being understood, and how communication can be improved. Feedback channels can include email, social media, collaboration tools, surveys, interviews, etc. The type of feedback and any need for privacy/anonymity will dictate which channel is used. Stakeholders who feel their feedback will be acted on are much more likely to engage in the feedback process. Anonymous feedback can be more challenging to implement in a collaborative way, as there is no way to discuss and clarify the feedback with the people submitting it.

5: Focus on organisational change management

> It's commonly accepted that most feedback comes from customers and users who have a strong opinion about your product or service. Whether they love it or hate it, they're more likely to contact you than someone who thinks 'meh, it was OK'. Think about what you're collecting the feedback for, and how it will shape the evolution of your product and service. You don't necessarily want to be making major changes just because one person hated the shade of blue that you chose. Feedback can be used in many ways – to build a relationship, to identify improvements, to validate a decision, or to identify opportunities to make a sale. If you're clear about WHY you're collecting feedback, how, where, when, etc. will come much more easily.

OCM throughout the service value chain

Information flows through the service value chain (SVC). If information flow is disrupted, the chain can be slowed or broken. The OCM practice methods can be used to establish and facilitate human interfaces across the value chain. This can reduce any frustration or resentment felt by people who aren't getting the information they need.

Interfaces across the value chain

Across the SVC and value streams, people need to be able to collaborate effectively. This is supported by the guiding principles 'collaborate and promote visibility' and 'think and

5: Focus on organisational change management

work holistically'. Clear interfaces need to be established and understood between all organisations and people involved in the value chain activities.

OCM methods and techniques can be used to help establish interfaces across the value chain. They can be used to examine the interfaces, understand the stakeholders involved and improve communication between activities.

Some good practices to follow when defining interfaces are:

- *"Encourage active stakeholder participation Users who have the authority and ability to provide information about the system and interfaces being built should be given the opportunity to do so.*
- *Review and approve It is important to review the interface and design documents for precision, comprehensiveness, and usability.*
- *Standardize Whenever possible, project teams should consider using an industry-recognized standard for system interfaces.*
- *Document clearly Interface details should be documented as interface control documents and supporting system specifications should be documented as system design documents.*
- *Have a clear rationale It is important to document the rationales behind design decisions and trade-offs.*
- *Understand other interfaces Systems and devices have varying interfaces. Understanding any required system interfaces prior to design is crucial.*
- *Verify It is important to ensure that all models fulfil their functional requirements.*

5: Focus on organisational change management

- ***Be aware of trade-offs** In most instances, there are several ways to accomplish something. It is important to consider the positives and negatives of each approach, and how their effects could propagate throughout the system."*

Internal and external partner relationships also need to be supported by effective interfaces. Open communication channels allow issues to be discussed and improvement opportunities identified. OCM methods and techniques can help establish clear, simple communication channels and processes. These will be the foundation of healthy relationships.

If you're ready to accept that you live in VUCA world, having effective OCM capabilities is essential. Review what OCM activities happen where in your organisation. Are there good practices to build on? Or obvious gaps to address? The assessment methods we studied in chapter 4 will be helpful here.

CHAPTER 6: DPI, MEASUREMENT AND REPORTING

Measurement and continual improvement are embedded in every element of IT and IT service management. Without measurement and analysis, we cannot make good decisions. Choosing what to improve, directing activities and validating success all rely on effective measurement and reporting.

It can be tempting to think of measurement as dull, administrative, routine work. It's anything but. Measuring the right things gives you a health check of your organisation, products, services, technology…and early warning when things are going wrong.

Measurement and reporting have moved beyond glossy monthly management packs. Try reading up on concepts like observability and how they relate to your role.

6: DPI, measurement and reporting

> "In the world of software products and services, observability means you can answer any questions about what's happening on the inside of the system just by observing the outside of the system, without having to ship new code to answer new questions. Observability is what we need our tools to deliver now that system complexity is outpacing our ability to predict what's going to break."[21]

Measurement and reporting basics

The measurement and reporting practice has a role across the SVS and supports DPI activities.

"The purpose of the measurement and reporting practice is to support good decision-making and continual improvement by reducing uncertainty. This is achieved by collecting relevant data and assessing it in appropriate contexts. Data can be collected on products, services, practices, value chain activities, teams, individuals, suppliers, partners, and the collective organization."

Organisations can only make improvements when they know where they are right now. Huge volumes of metrics can be generated by IT products and services. The service provider must ensure it is measuring the right things and not wasting effort. Metrics need to provide data that supports effective decision-making across the four dimensions of service management.

A **measurement** is *"a means of decreasing uncertainty based on one or more observations that are expressed in*

---

[21] *https://docs.honeycomb.io/learning-about-observability/intro-to-observability/*.

6: DPI, measurement and reporting

quantifiable units". Measurement provides data that can be processed into metrics.

A **metric** is *"a measurement or calculation that is monitored or reported for management and improvement"*. Metrics need to provide meaningful information and support decision-making. Important metrics can be associated with objectives and used as indicators.

An **indicator** is *"a metric that is used to assess and manage something"*. Indicators should have a target trend and value assigned to them. There may also be a tolerance range for deviations from the target. Indicators can be aggregated for analysis. The information is often presented to relevant stakeholders on dashboards and reports.

A **report** is *"a detailed communication of information or knowledge about a topic or event"*. Reports will be organised and presented in the most relevant way for their target audience. They can be prepared on demand, or at agreed intervals (or both). Reports need to be accurate, complete and well-organised. They need to be reviewed regularly to ensure they are still relevant and necessary.

Many organisations measure too much. They drown in data, making it hard to see what really matters. A better approach is to start with a minimum set of data and build out from it as different needs are identified. Each element of the SVS needs to be measured to show the value it is creating and how it can be improved. Measurements should be regularly reviewed and will need to be updated if the organisation changes its vision or mission.

6: DPI, measurement and reporting

Reasons for measuring

Measurements need to be aligned with the organisation's objectives and will guide DPI activities. There are four main reasons to measure:

- To validate
- To influence
- To justify
- To intervene

> ❓
>
> Why not assess the measurements you report against (and the reports you receive) and decide if they meet any of these four reasons? If they don't, why are you producing or receiving the reports? Is it just a habit?

Table 21 provides more detail.

6: DPI, measurement and reporting

Table 21: Four Key Reasons to Measure[22]

Reason	Explanation
To validate	By measuring achievement against targets or objectives, past decisions can be validated.
To influence	By defining measurable targets, an organization sets the direction for activities, and sets expectations for outcomes. It is important to understand how each metric influences people, as the effect of a measurement on behaviour and expectations is not always what was intended.
To justify	Use metrics to justify with evidence or proof that a course of action is required. For example, metrics produced to support a business case.

---

[22] *ITIL® 4: Direct, Plan and Improve*, table 4.1. Copyright © AXELOS Limited 2020.

6: DPI, measurement and reporting

To intervene	Measurements can be used to pre-emptively identify a point of intervention, including for subsequent changes and corrective actions.

Figure 8 shows the four key reasons to measure.

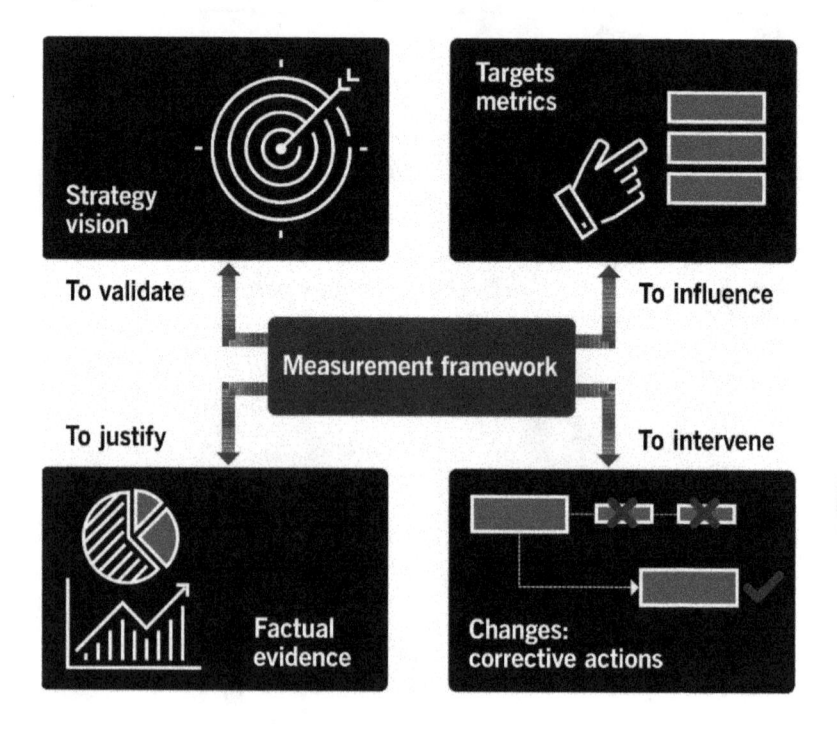

Figure 8: Four key reasons to measure[23]

---

[23] *ITIL® 4: Direct, Plan and Improve*, figure 4.1. Copyright © AXELOS Limited 2020.

6: DPI, measurement and reporting

Types of measurements

There are five broad types of measurements:

- Progress
- Compliance
- Effectiveness
- Efficiency
- Productivity

Table 22 shows some examples.

Table 22: Types of Measurements[24]

Measurement Type	Description	Examples
Progress	*Progress measurements demonstrate the degree of achievement relative to defined milestones and/or deliverables. They may be seen as indicators of*	*Percentage of unit tests executed and passed* *Percentage of use cases with completed documentation*

---

[24] *ITIL® 4: Direct, Plan and Improve*, table 4.2. Copyright © AXELOS Limited 2020.

6: DPI, measurement and reporting

	something's degree of completeness.	
Compliance	Compliance measurements demonstrate the degree of adherence to governance and/or regulatory requirements.	Percentage of changes executed without prior authorization Number of non-compliance audit findings
Effectiveness	Effectiveness measurements demonstrate the degree of fitness for purpose of any part of the SVS, a product, or a service.	Number of broken links on the public customer order website Percentage of failed payment transactions
Efficiency	Efficiency measurements demonstrate the degree of fitness for use of any part of the SVS, a	Percentage of services meeting their availability targets Percentage reduction in processing time

6: DPI, measurement and reporting

	product, or a service.	for loan application
Productivity	Productivity measurements demonstrate the throughput of a system (a value stream, a process, a service, a component) over a period of time.	Number of tasks fulfilled by a team Number of customers served at a supermarket cash register

> You'll notice none of the reasons to measure or types of measurements refer to 'finding someone to blame' or 'finding something to shout at our suppliers about'. I've worked with several organisations that use measurements and metrics as a punishment tool, rather than a way of identifying new opportunities and improvements. Effective products and services rely on collaboration, shared knowledge and good relationships between stakeholders. Using reports as a way to punish people only encourages people to submit inaccurate reports.

6: DPI, measurement and reporting

Measurement and behaviour

Measuring can direct behaviour, positively or negatively. Organisations need to anticipate how a measurement might affect behaviour so they can plan for any impact. Measurement and reporting should be used to provide information and drive improvement, not to place blame. If employees think they will be blamed for something going wrong, they might try to hide information.

Measurement cascades and hierarchies

Metrics and measures need to be aligned with the organisation's objectives, vision and mission. There are several approaches that support this alignment:

- Planning and evaluation model.
- Balanced scorecard.
- IT component-to-scorecard hierarchy.
- Organisational improvement cascade.

Planning and evaluation model

Figure 9 shows the planning and evaluation model. It connects the organisation's purpose to the metrics being measured. The model can be used to determine metrics for all sorts of activities. It also relates to the ITIL guiding principles. For example, 'progress iteratively with feedback' – feedback from lower levels of the model can be used to ensure that planning is realistic. Or perhaps 'think and work holistically' – the model helps to show a range of metrics that can provide a holistic view of success.

6: DPI, measurement and reporting

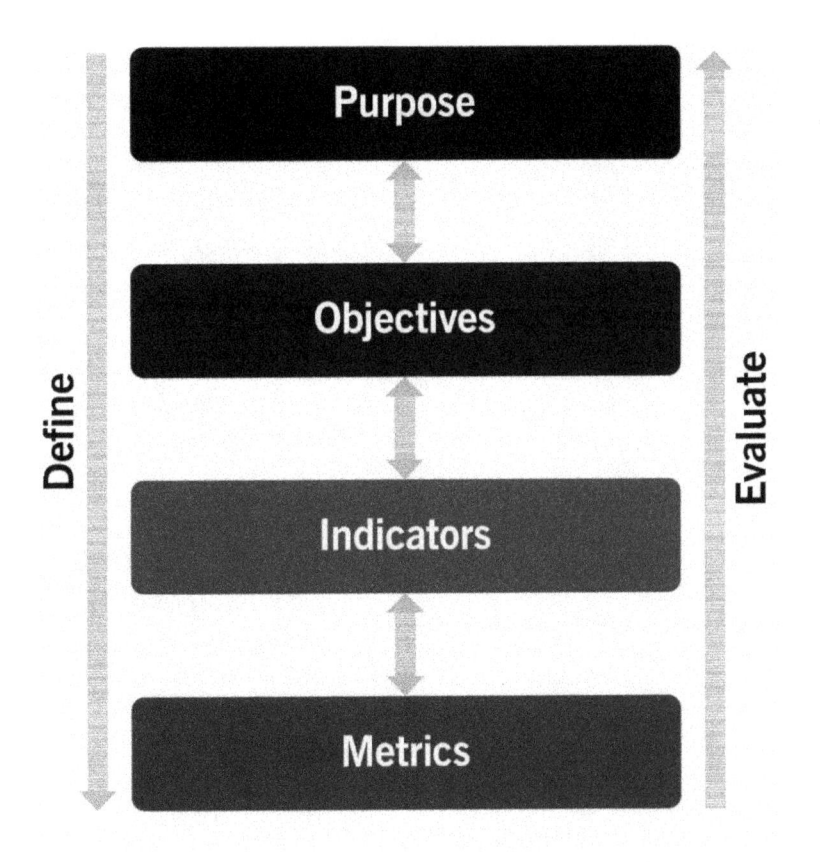

Figure 9: The planning and evaluation model[25]

Table 23 also provides more information.

---

[25] *ITIL® 4: Direct, Plan and Improve*, figure 4.2. Copyright © AXELOS Limited 2020.

6: DPI, measurement and reporting

Table 23: The Planning and Evaluation Model Levels[26]

Term	Questions answered	Practical application
Purpose	Why are we doing this?	This is where the core mission is articulated. Everything needed to achieve and validate the mission can be determined from this high-level purpose. The purpose should be defined at the appropriate level. It should be specific enough to define the associated objectives.

---

[26] *ITIL® 4: Direct, Plan and Improve*, table 4.3. Copyright © AXELOS Limited 2020.

6: DPI, measurement and reporting

Objectives	What would a successful result look like? What are the characteristics of success?	Objectives are used to define what should be achieved or created to ensure that the desired purpose will be fulfilled. They refine the defined purpose into specifics. There will typically be several objectives associated with the purpose, each of which will need to be acted on, with the results of that action being measured.
Indicators	What measurable results would indicate success? How many different indicators are needed for effective evaluation?	To evaluate the achievement of objectives, a balanced set of indicators should be defined based on relevant

6: DPI, measurement and reporting

		metrics. For each objective, there will be at least one, but more likely several, measurable elements that will indicate the degree of success in achieving what was desired.
		An indicator is typically based on one or more metrics, each one associated with a desired trend or target.
		Indicators should not be treated as objectives; their effects on people's behaviour should always be considered.

6: DPI, measurement and reporting

Metrics	*What are the numbers?* *How many per period?* *How long per issue?* *What percentage of all items recorded?*	*Metrics are used to collect data for evaluation and assessment. It is important to ensure that this data is relevant, accurate, reliable, and up to date.* *Every indicator is based on one or more metrics, but not every metric contributes to an indicator.*

Balanced scorecard

The balanced scorecard can be used to measure four perspectives that contribute to the overall organisational mission. It looks at:

- **Customers**, which measures areas including customer experience and satisfaction;
- **Financial**, including traditional financial management;
- **Internal** (business process), measures that provide a good leading indicator of future performance; and
- **Innovation** (learning and growth), measures that are linked to continual improvement.

6: DPI, measurement and reporting

Metrics are developed for each area of the scorecard, providing a balanced view. To support the balanced scorecard, the key performance indicators used will:

- Prove whether a strategy is working;
- Show the degree of performance change over time;
- Focus attention on the things that matter for success;
- Allow the measurement of accomplishments, not effort;
- Provide a common language for communication; and
- Reduce uncertainty.

> Do the reports you have access to provide a holistic viewpoint, or are they focused on a single area? Many technical teams focus on measuring technology, and don't look at the wider context for their products and services.

IT component-to-scorecard hierarchy

IT components can be measured to build a picture of overall service performance or to contribute to a balanced scorecard. However, these may not provide a full picture of the customer journey or experience.

Some organisations are using eXperience level agreements (XLAs) to complement traditional IT metrics.

6: DPI, measurement and reporting

Organisational improvement cascade

Organisations need to measure performance at multiple levels, typically including:

- Organisation
- Business units
- Departments
- Teams
- Individuals

Each level needs its own, appropriate, metrics. The objectives at each level should support objectives at higher levels, cascading up to support the organisation's overall mission. Improvements can be identified at each level, leading to a hierarchy of improvement plans. Figure 10 shows the improvement cascade.

6: DPI, measurement and reporting

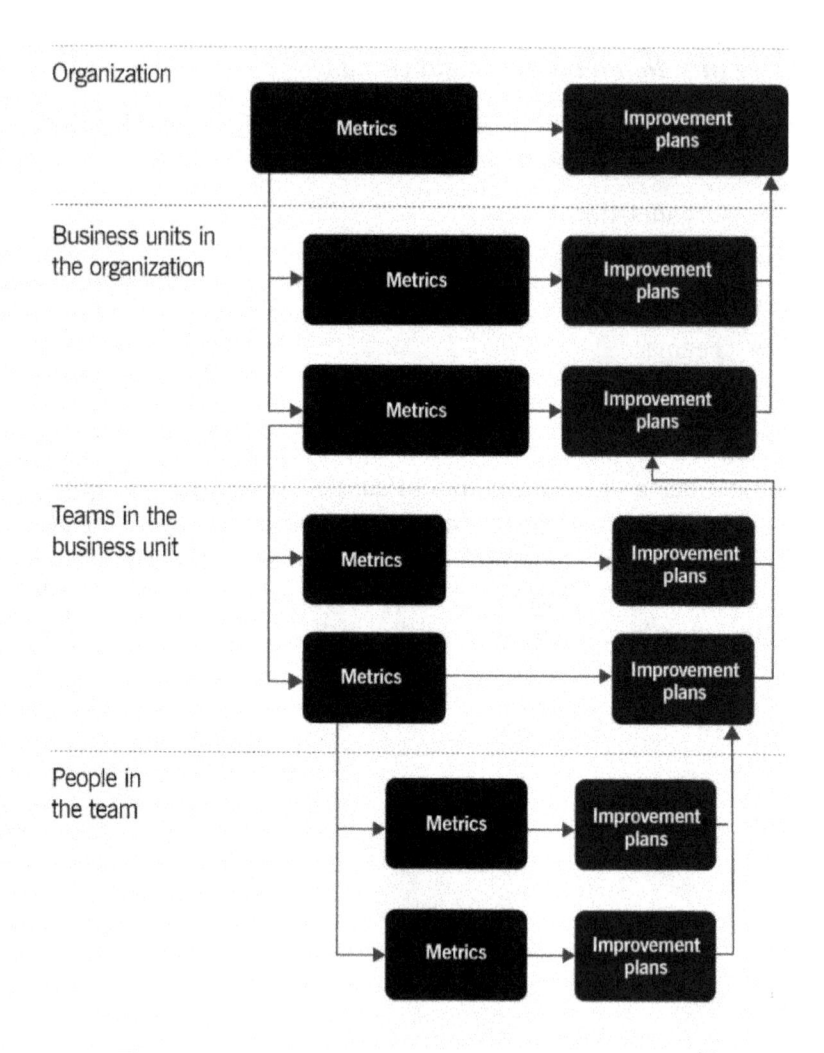

Figure 10: Organisational improvement cascade[27]

---

[27] *ITIL® 4: Direct, Plan and Improve*, figure 4.3. Copyright © AXELOS Limited 2020.

6: DPI, measurement and reporting

> At Banksbest, Lucy Jones is testing biometrics as part of the My Way project. What metrics could she use to measure the technical solution, the customer response to the solution and its alignment with business goals?

Success factors and KPIs

"A success factor describes a condition or characteristic that must be achieved for something to be considered successful. When the success factor relates to an ITIL practice, it is called a practice success factor (PSF)."

Each ITIL practice has a set of success factors, which help to express what the practice is intended to achieve. Each PSF is measured and validated using key performance indicators (KPIs).

KPIs are used to indicate the fulfilment of a success factor. For example, one of the OCM PSFs is to *"create and maintain a change enabling culture"*. This could be measured with KPIs such as:

- Attitude to organisational change across the organisation;
- Level of resistance to changes; and
- Awareness of the OCM practice across the organisation.

6: DPI, measurement and reporting

SMART

Many organisations use SMART indicators. These are:

- Specific
- Measurable
- Achievable
- Relevant
- Time-bound

> SMART sounds pretty simple and obvious – a little bit like 'KISS' – keep it simple, stupid! However, like many obvious things, it's not always that easy. Check some of the indicators that apply to your role, and your team's objectives. Are any of them SMART? Look out for warning signals such as:
>
> - We want to be better at... (how much better?);
> - Soon, we will...(when?); and
> - We'll do this twice as fast... (with what staff or resources!?).

Table 24 shows more detail about SMART.

6: DPI, measurement and reporting

Table 24: The SMART Model[28]

Abbr.	Criteria	Explanation
S	*Specific*	*Clarity on what is needed or intended is critical. The factor being evaluated must be defined in such a way that there is very little room for misinterpretation or misunderstanding.*
M	*Measurable*	*It should be possible, either directly or indirectly, to measure the factor being evaluated. For a metric, this concept seems clear and the measurement is direct. In some cases, the only way to 'measure' an objective is by critically analysing associated indicators.*

---

[28] *ITIL® 4: Direct, Plan and Improve*, table 4.6. Copyright © AXELOS Limited 2020.

6: DPI, measurement and reporting

A	*Achievable*	*Setting an unrealistic objective is unproductive. Those working towards the objective must believe that it is achievable if they are to maintain their commitment and focus.*
R	*Relevant*	*Any factor being evaluated must make sense relative to desired outcomes.*
T	*Time-bound*	*Everyone involved should understand the timeframe for achieving the factor being evaluated. A measurement or metric defined in alignment with the SMART method should not be open-ended.*

CHAPTER 7: DPI, VALUE STREAMS AND PRACTICES

An important part of building your own capabilities to direct, plan and improve is understanding how to direct, plan and improve value streams and practices, including:

- The differences between value streams and practices, and how those differences affect DPI; and
- How to select and use appropriate methods and practices:
  - Addressing the four dimensions.
  - Applying the guiding principles.
  - Value stream mapping.
  - Optimisation of workflow.
  - Elimination of waste.
  - Ensuring and utilising feedback.

Value streams and processes in the Service Value System

Service management workflows can be visualised, organised and improved by using value streams. Organisations need to identify and map value streams, to allow them to analyse their current state. Value stream analysis can identify barriers, bottlenecks and wasteful, low-value activities. An organisation might start by mapping value streams related to a service that is not performing well, or it might start with its most valuable service. Over time, more value streams can be created as they are needed.

7: DPI, value streams and practices

Value streams provide a way for value to be delivered to customers. Each step adds value to the unit of work being processed, changing demand and opportunities into valuable outcomes. Each step in a value stream is defined and will use one or more ITIL practices. ITIL focuses on optimising value streams, at each step and as a collection of steps.

Analysing value streams allows organisations to identify improvements to value streams and the practices they use. This combines a Lean approach to flow optimisation and elimination of waste with ITIL's guiding principles:

- Focus on value.
- Think and work holistically.
- Progress iteratively with feedback.

Value stream mapping is *"a Lean management technique to visualize the steps needed to convert demand into value, used to identify opportunities to improve"*.

Map a value stream for something that you offer to your customers and users. Look at any bottlenecks or delays, or redundant steps. Value stream mapping is a powerful tool to support many of the areas we've looked at in this book. It can really help to start a conversation with stakeholders, identify improvements and increase communication. This is an area I'd recommend you do more detailed reading on

7: DPI, value streams and practices

> after you complete your DPI studies. There are some great case studies and examples available online.

Value streams and practices

Service management needs to focus on more than just processes. Processes support value co-creation and are not a valuable outcome on their own. ITIL 4 helps organisations focus on value and value streams, supported by the ITIL practices, and addressing all four dimensions of service management. Figure 11[29] shows the relationship between a value stream and practices. Value chain activities are building blocks for value streams, supported by practices.

---

[29] *ITIL® 4: Direct, Plan and Improve*, figure 7.3. Copyright © AXELOS Limited 2020.

7: DPI, value streams and practices

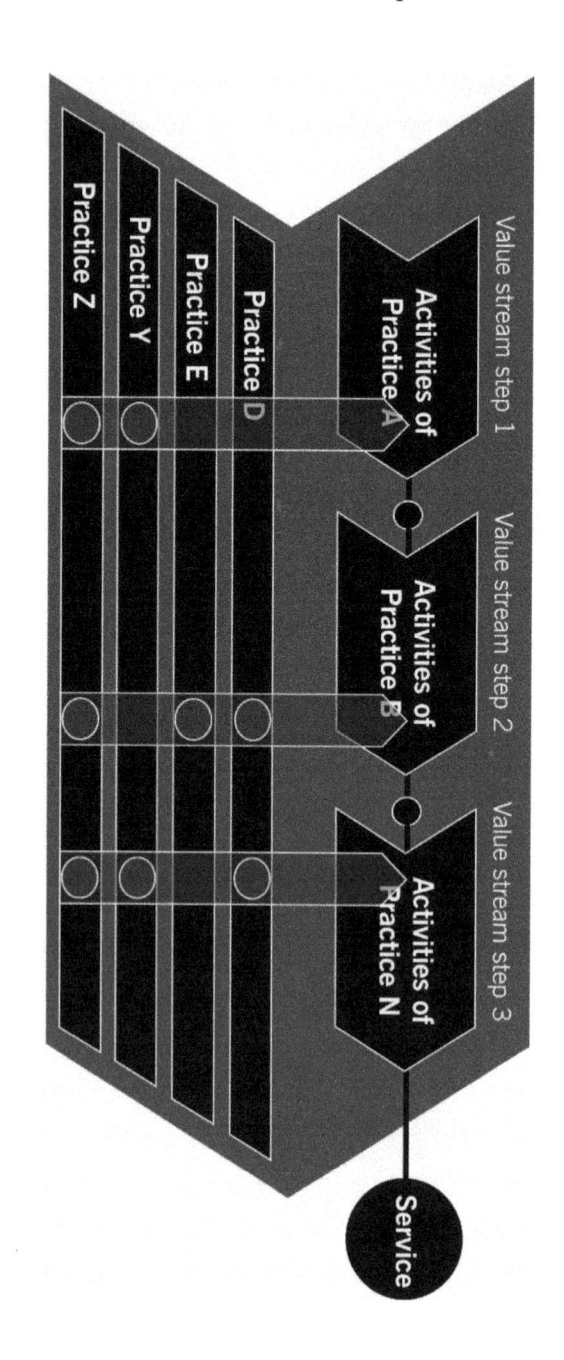

Figure 11: The relationship between value streams and practices

7: DPI, value streams and practices

Value streams and processes

While they are not the same, value streams and processes do have common elements, including:

- Focus on activities and workflow;
- Provide an organisation with a view of what happens, and how; and
- Defined activities, inputs and outputs.

Both value streams and processes can be mapped for analysis.

The main differences between value streams and processes are their focus areas and how they are used. Value streams focus on a flow of activity from demand or opportunity to value. Processes describe interrelated activities that transform inputs into outputs.

> IT service management (and ITIL) have been perceived in the past by some IT practitioners as too process-driven and bureaucratic. Whatever your view on the truth of this (in my view, it's unwarranted), it's important to avoid 'process for process's sake'. ITIL 4 uses practices as a more holistic concept, addressing the roles, capabilities and principles as well as the processes and procedures required to be successful in areas like change management and incident management. This doesn't, however, mean process is dead. Processes are valuable ways of

7: DPI, value streams and practices

> documenting and improving repeated tasks that deliver outcomes. Once a process is defined, it can be carried out consistently and, possibly, automated. Processes can free up organisational thinking space for more complex activities.

Measurement and the four dimensions

Without measurement, organisations cannot understand their current position and where improvements need to be made. Improvements that are made based on perception or gut instinct are less likely to deliver valuable outcomes.

Organisations and people

This dimension includes roles and responsibilities, organisational structures, culture, staffing and competencies. Measurements include:

- Team performance;
- Staff retention;
- Training;
- Net promoter score ('how likely are you to recommend working here?'); and
- Any other relevant metrics.

Information and technology

Technology components are usually easy to measure, but it can be challenging to identify what is important. Measurements should provide value and be relevant. This dimension also includes information and knowledge needed to manage services. Organisations must be able to manage the enabling technologies for all of the four dimensions.

7: DPI, value streams and practices

When a service has many users (for example, SaaS offerings), technology performance measures can be aggregated and used as a proxy for user experience. This allows improvements to be identified without direct contact with users.

Partners and suppliers

Service providers need to create a collaborative relationship with their suppliers and partners, which are often an essential part of service provision. Organisations and their suppliers should want each other to be successful. Service level agreements and contracts are often used to measure their performance. SLA targets need to be regularly reviewed to ensure they are still valid.

Partner and supplier relationships can also be measured through:

- Compliance with applicable regulations;
- Conformance to service agreement terms and conditions;
- Social responsibility; and
- Assurance of the supplier's reliability and flexibility as customer needs change.

Looking at the Banksbest case study, what measurements would be particularly important for Mortbank? If you

7: DPI, value streams and practices

> were managing the relationship with this supplier, what improvements would you want to see? Think about areas including communication as well as simply 'better service'.

Value streams and processes

Measuring value streams and processes will highlight bottlenecks and blocks, to allow improvements to be identified. Value streams and process measures include:

Table 25: Value stream and process measures

Lagging and leading indicators	Lagging and leading indicators help organisations understand their past performance and predict future trends. Senior managers often request historical information, but they also need to be able to predict future performance in order to build a vision to direct, plan and improve. • Lagging indicators report what has been achieved. • Leading indicators predict the future. Leading indicators can be influenced by service provider actions.

7: DPI, value streams and practices

Process metrics	New processes are measured to judge how well they are established and if they are being carried out (compliance). As a process matures, the measurement focus switches to effectiveness and efficiency. Is the process delivering the required outputs? After this, the process can be gradually improved.
Flow efficiency	Flow metrics can help analyse how efficient a process is. They include: • Work in progress (WIP) – a measure of unfinished work items. • Cycle time – the time between work starting and finishing. This is a lagging indicator of flow. • Throughput – a measure of the number of work items finished in a period of time. Work item age – how long active items are in progress. This is a leading indicator for unfinished items.

7: DPI, value streams and practices

Table 26: Using the guiding principles for DPI

Focus on value	This principle focuses on value creation for all stakeholders. It is closely aligned to DPI, and the organisation's vision and mission should be used to provide direction during value stream design. Organisations need governance systems and actionable strategies to realise value. For each decision, they must ask: • Who will receive the benefits? • Who bears the risk? • What resources are required?
Start where you are	DPI isn't just about brand-new products, services and processes. Existing resources and projects can also add value. Assessment methods should be used to analyse the current state and identify what value streams, practices, products and

7: DPI, value streams and practices

	services can be re-used or improved.
Progress iteratively with feedback	Trying to do too much at once can lead to overload. Large improvement initiatives should be broken down into smaller sections. The overall improvement plan needs to be constantly reassessed to ensure it is still aligned with the organisation's vision and mission.
Collaborate and promote visibility	Organisations that work in siloes cannot make holistic improvements. It is important to support collaboration and cooperation between all teams and across the four dimensions of service management. Visibility helps people understand the bigger picture, allowing them to prioritise more effectively.
Think and work holistically	Organisations need to manage holistically, rather

7: DPI, value streams and practices

	than focusing on individual activities. DPI should support a holistic approach. The four dimensions of service management and the service value system help to support the holistic view.
Keep it simple and practical	If something isn't providing value, it should be eliminated. Value streams should use the minimum number of steps to accomplish objectives, and then exceptions should be managed using rules and guidelines. It's not efficient to create a solution for every exception. To apply this principle: • Ensure value from every activity; • Leverage simplicity and focus on doing fewer things better; • Respect people's time and intelligence; • Make things easy to understand and adopt; and • Maximise quick wins.

7: DPI, value streams and practices

Optimise and automate	Optimisation is the action of making the best or most effective use of a situation or resource. Automation refers to the use of technology to perform activities with little to no human intervention. Direction, planning and improvement can help identify a strategy for optimisation and automation, and provide guidance about where it can be appropriately applied.

> The guiding principles are an important part of ITIL 4. The suggestion of the ITIL 4 authors is that you print them out and display them in your workplace to help guide decision-making. Why not create your own guiding principles poster?

Ensuring and using feedback

Direction, planning and improvement doesn't take place in a vacuum. Service providers need feedback. The guiding principles can help to support the collection and processing of feedback, as can many of the activities that we've studied, including:

- Communication; and
- Defining and establishing feedback channels.

Feedback can help identify whether a change is 'sticking' or not. Service providers need to be sure that staff don't revert back to old ways of working. When the desired state is maintained, this is referred to as **'institutionalising'** the change.

Value stream mapping

Value stream mapping is a Lean technique that helps to visualise the flow from demand or opportunity to value. The flow can be studied, and improvements identified.

Value stream mapping can identify which activities are adding value (or not!), and allow the organisation to make improvements and work towards its desired future state. Value streams can extend outside the organisation to partners, suppliers and consumer organisations.

Lean

Lean focuses on maximising customer value while minimising waste. It creates more value with fewer resources. Waste should be eliminated, and technology used to its maximum potential. Lean aims to provide perfect value, through a perfect value creation process with no waste. It encourages management to focus on optimising flow, not separate technologies, or activities.

7: DPI, value streams and practices

> I once heard someone argue that the service desk is an example of waste. Why bother having the customer contact a service desk team member? Why not route the customers directly to a skilled technical resource who can answer any challenging questions immediately? It's a valid argument, but there are also many counter-arguments (the expense of skilled resource, the comfort for the customer in having a defined escalation path, the percentage of service enquiries that actually require technical skills...). As with any methodology, framework or standard, look at what Lean says and balance it against the environment you work in, and your common sense.

Local optimisation

Many organisations focus on local optimisation of a single activity or process step. This can actually make things worse by creating bottlenecks in other areas. Optimisation should focus on the flow of work. Value stream maps can help to visualise the flow of work.

Benefits of value stream mapping

Value stream mapping adds value because it:

- *"Helps organizations to visualize more than the single-process level in production*
- *Helps organizations to identify and remove waste*

7: DPI, value streams and practices

- *Highlights where decisions about workflow need to be discussed and made*
- *Incorporates Lean concepts and techniques*
- *Helps to plan and document improvements"*

Developing a value stream map

To develop a value stream map, these steps need to be followed:

- Document the current way of working (create a baseline).
- Identify waste activities.
- Identify improvements.
- Map the direct future state, focusing on identifying waste and improving flow.

It's good practice to involve the people who carry out the work in the mapping exercise. The improvements identified during value stream mapping should be implemented in an agreed time frame. Many organisations keep this time frame short to allow for quick progress and to build momentum. Improvements that will take more than three months to implement can be broken down into smaller initiatives. Value maps are iterative and will be updated as the work progresses.

Tables 27 and 28 provide more information.

7: DPI, value streams and practices

Table 27: Types of Waste[30]

Waste Type	Meaning
Muda	*Waste, uselessness, futility. Things that are being done but which add no value.*
Muri	*Overburden, excessiveness, or unreasonableness. Caused by rigid service timeframes, release windows, and other such time constraints.*
Mura	*Variability, unevenness, non-uniformity, irregularity. Unacceptable variation or impediments in ways of working or workflows.*

Table 28: Muda subcategories[31]

Waste Type	Description
Transport of goods	Movement of work product, information, materials

---

[30] *ITIL® 4: Direct, Plan and Improve*, table 3.17. Copyright © AXELOS Limited 2020.
[31] *ITIL® 4: Direct, Plan and Improve*, table 3.18. Copyright © AXELOS Limited 2020.

7: DPI, value streams and practices

Inventory	Work in progress, having more than strategic levels of products
Motion of people	Unnecessary physical movement
Waiting time	Stopping or slowing down, waiting for work to arrive
Overproduction	Producing more than is needed or before it is needed
Over processing	Excessive or unnecessary work
Defects and rework	Reworking to correct mistakes, inspection, and scrap
Talent	Unused human creativity and potential

7: DPI, value streams and practices

> **?**
>
> Can you find examples of each of these types of waste in your organisation?

Value stream maps need to be specific enough to support detailed analysis. Detail and clarity need to be in balance – too much information, and the map becomes confusing and difficult to analyse. Figure 12 shows some of the figures that can be added to maps to make them clearer. Different symbols are used to highlight information flows and physical flows. The Kaizen burst is used to highlight an area where more investigation is needed.

7: DPI, value streams and practices

Waste symbols		Other symbols	
🚚	Transport of goods	- - - -▶	Information flow
⚠	Inventory	⟶	Physical flow
🚶	Motion of people	🏭	External supplier
⏱	Waiting time	⬇	Process/process step
🖥	Overprocessing	✴	Kaizen burst
⬆	Overproduction		
🔄	Defects and rework		

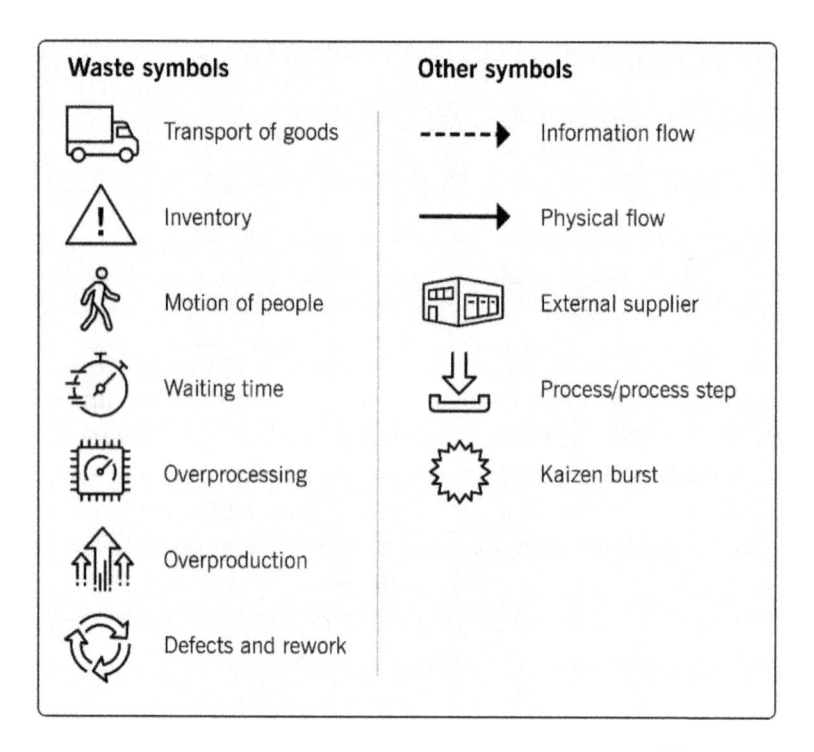

Figure 12: Value stream mapping symbols[32]

Workflow optimisation

Value stream mapping and the process measures we studied in previous sections can be used to support workflow optimisation:

- Leading and lagging indicators.
- Process metrics.
- Flow efficiency.

---

[32] *ITIL® 4: Direct, Plan and Improve*, figure 3.2. Copyright © AXELOS Limited 2020.

7: DPI, value streams and practices

Focus questions can be used to design workflows for a process or value stream. They include:

- *"What will cause the work to start?*
- *What information, whether it is obtained from an external stakeholder or internally, is required to create the defined outputs or outcomes? When will the information be available? What format will the information be in?*
- *Which steps need to occur in order to achieve the required output? Which steps can be performed in parallel and which have prerequisite steps, activities, or sub-processes? How long does each step take?*
- *What artefacts are created by the workflow?*
- *What value does each step create for the service provider, its consumers, or other stakeholders?*
- *Which policies must the process or value stream comply with?*
- *What aspects of the workflow will be measured? How will the data be formatted, stored, and used?"*

Considerations for efficient design

Process design can be supported by templates and toolkits, either freely available or provided by vendors, consultants and trainers. These can provide a good start point but need to be adapted to meet the needs of the organisation. Metrics also need to be defined for each workflow or activity. Figure 13[33] shows the metrics, based on Little's Law.

---

[33] *ITIL® 4: Direct, Plan and Improve*, figure 7.4. Copyright © AXELOS Limited 2020.

7: DPI, value streams and practices

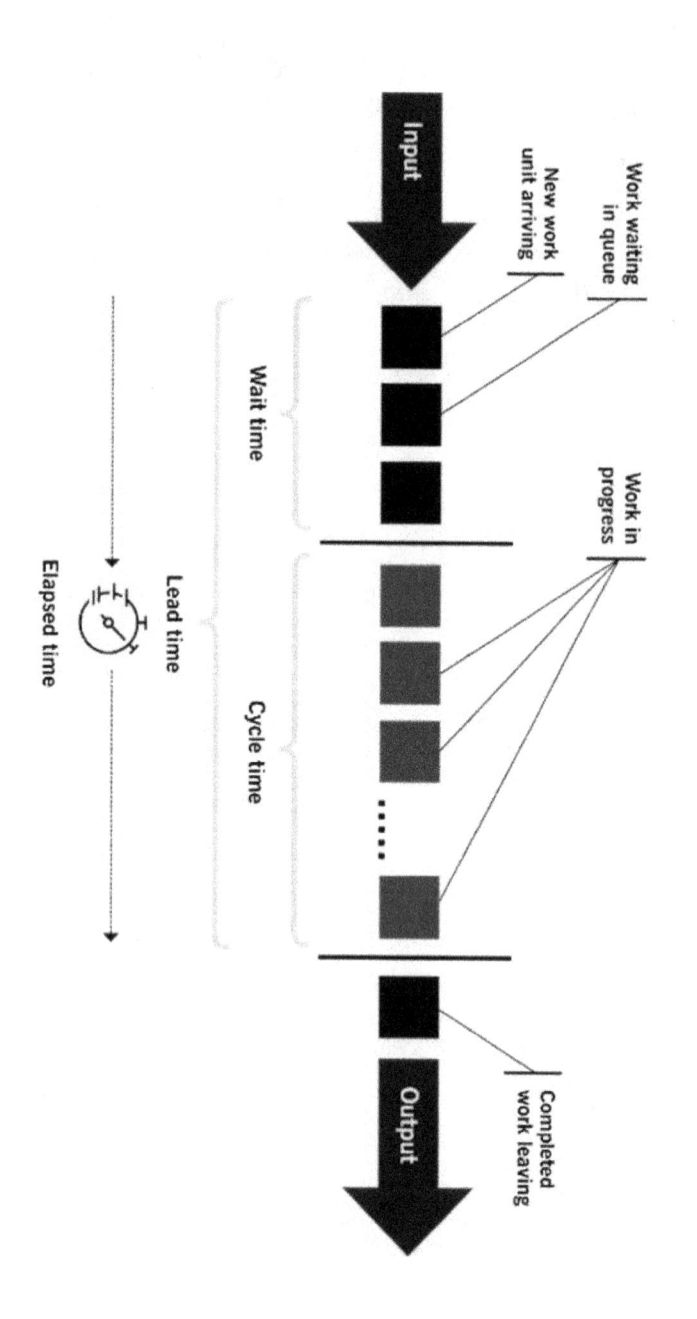

Figure 13: Process timing

7: DPI, value streams and practices

Little's Law provides some considerations for process design:

- Minimise how often work is transferred.
- Throughput may not be under the service provider's control.
- Wait time can be expressed as a function of cycle time.
- Cycle time can be assumed to be fixed.
- WIP can be limited to stabilise cycle time.

Theory of constraints

The theory of constraints provides another perspective on process flows; we mentioned this earlier when we studied local optimisation. There is a five-step process to apply this theory:

- Identify the process's constraints.
- Decide how best to exploit the process's constraints.
- Subordinate everything else to the above decisions.
- Evaluate the process's constraints.
- Remove the constraints and re-evaluate the process.

> The Theory of Constraints was introduced in *The Goal*, a business novel by Eliyahu M. Goldratt and Jeff Cox. Put simply, the Theory of Constraints recognises that every

7: DPI, value streams and practices

> process has a point that has the potential to be a bottleneck.
>
> To function more efficiently, organisations need to identify constraints and reduce the impact of the bottleneck or remove it completely. Not all constraints can be eliminated, but their effects can be reduced. For example, a regulatory requirement might create a constraint that cannot be completely eliminated.
>
> *The Phoenix Project* was written as a homage to *The Goal*. It is described as "A Novel About IT, DevOps, and Helping Your Business Win". One of the authors, Gene Kim, explained in *Beyond the Phoenix Project*: "Our hope was that, in The Phoenix Project, we could describe in equal clarity every sort of problem that every functional silo in the technology value stream also faced."
>
> I would definitely recommend adding *The Goal* and *The Phoenix Project* to your reading list to help you understand value systems, constraints and the challenges associated with providing IT services in an environment that requires both speed and safety.

Kanban

Kanban is a method of work that pulls the flow of work through a process at a manageable pace while reducing work in progress. Kanban is a 'pull' system, allowing teams to pull work in only when they are ready for it – reducing overburden. Kanban is designed to reduce idle time and waste in a process.

In Japanese, Kan means visual and Ban means card. Visual cards are used to trigger action, allowing teams to pull work

7: DPI, value streams and practices

when they are ready for it and people to work collaboratively to improve flow.

A basic Kanban board has columns for To Do, In Progress and Done.

- **To Do:** Kanban makes work visible. Teams can see what needs to be done and pull work when they have the capacity to do it.
- **In Progress:** Work in progress, or WIP, needs to be limited to the capacity of the resources available. Too much WIP can lead to overburden. You might experience this yourself on a personal level. Some days there seems to be so much to do, it's hard to start anything. Kanban helps to visualise and manage workflow.
- **Done:** Kanban can be used to measure velocity – the quantity of work completed in an iteration or sprint. Lead time and cycle time can be measured using the boards. Kanban doesn't have to be complex to implement. It can be as simple as sticky notes on a wall, or a whiteboard.

CHAPTER 8: EXAM PREPARATION

Here are the key facts about the ITIL 4 DPI exam:

- The exam is 90 minutes. Extra time is allowable if English is not your native language and a translated paper isn't available.
- The exam is closed book – it's just you and your knowledge.
- It has 40 multiple-choice questions, and you must get 28 correct, or 70%, to pass.
- There is no negative marking (so you don't lose a mark if you get a question wrong).
- There are 13 questions at Bloom's Level 2 and 27 at Bloom's Level 3.

Remember that this is a Strategist course, and is part of both the Managing Professional and Strategic Leader streams.

Your training provider for DPI will provide you with access to at least one sample exam. When you're ready to attempt the sample paper, try to reproduce, as far as possible, the conditions of the real exam.

Set aside 90 minutes to complete the paper and make sure there are no distractions: don't make a coffee; don't raid the fridge; don't check your emails … or Facebook … or Twitter; switch off your phone.

If you don't focus exclusively on the sample exam questions, you will not have a good indication of your possible

8: Exam preparation

performance in the live exam. Your sample exam may highlight areas for further study before you take your final exam.

> Here are some good practices for taking multiple-choice exams:
>
> **Manage your time:** if you're stuck on a question, mark it and go back to it later. It's easy to spend too long staring at one question, but there may be easier marks to be picked up further on in the paper.
>
> **Have a technique:** I like to go through an exam and complete all the questions I feel confident about. That allows me to see how many of the more challenging ones I need to get right to have a successful result.
>
> **Trust your instinct:** one of the most common bits of exam feedback is candidates who wish they had not changed their answer at the last minute. It's fine to check over what you've done, but be very wary about making changes in those last few seconds.
>
> **Use the process of elimination:** each question has four possible answers – if you can discount one or two of them then you've dramatically increased your odds of picking the right answer.
>
> **Don't panic!:** if your mind goes blank, move on, and look at another question – you can do this with online and paper

8: Exam preparation

exams. Your subconscious mind will work away even when you're answering a different question.

Read the question carefully: if you're not careful, you will answer the question you **think** you see, not the one that's actually there.

And that's all from me! I hope you've enjoyed the book, and that the extra content I've provided along the way will help you to start using ITIL 4 DPI concepts in your own role. You can find me on LinkedIn and Twitter – I'd love to hear if you've enjoyed the book and how your studies and exam help you in your career.

APPENDIX: BANKSBEST CASE STUDY

Company overview

Banksbest was originally HW Banking. It was founded in 1953 in the UK and has branches in most major UK cities. It focuses mainly on business clients, but it also has a mortgage department that offers residential mortgages to aspiring homeowners and buy-to-let mortgages to landlords.

The Banksbest board of directors initiated a digital transformation programme in 2017. At the same time, a new CEO and CIO were recruited. A Chief Digital Officer (CDO) role has also been established. As part of the digital transformation programme, the bank rebranded from HW Banking to Banksbest, which was seen as a more customer-focused brand.

Banksbest has defined these strategic goals:

- To be the tenth largest provider of business banking services in the UK (growing its customer base by approximately 25%).
- To grow its residential mortgage business by 50%.
- To build a reputation as a 'digital first' banking provider.

There is some conflict during board meetings, as the CFO is not fully convinced about the value of the CDO role and the digital transformation programme. She would prefer to focus on cost management.

The head office and data centre for Banksbest are in Manchester. The customer service centre is in Reading. There is also an agreement with a business process

Appendix: Banksbest case study

outsourcing company in Bulgaria, Employeez on Demand, which provides additional customer service resources during peak times. The customer service centre operates 7 days a week, between 8:00 am and 6:00 pm, and support is also available via the bank's website on a 24x7 basis.

Banksbest's 50 branches are open Monday to Saturday, between 9:00 am and 5:00 pm.

Banksbest has a good reputation in a competitive field. However, the rebrand has confused some customers, and the digital transformation programme has not delivered many measurable results yet. Banksbest needs to improve its online services and embed its new brand in order to grow.

Company structure

Banksbest employs 700 staff. 400 work in the bank's branches, 100 in the call centre, and 200 in the head office and support functions. Additional staff are supplied by Employeez on Demand during peak times.

Banksbest is split into divisions:

- Central Operations – provides support services for all departments. Operations includes HR, Finance, Marketing and IT. The IT department has 50 staff.
- Customer Services – this department includes the staff who work in and manage the customer service centre, as well as some technical specialists who work on the systems used in the CS centre.
- Branches – this department is responsible for the branches providing face-to-face banking services. The branches are expensive to maintain but offer a face-to-face service that some Banksbest customers value.

Appendix: Banksbest case study

The digital transformation programme is being run by a digital team that operates outside the existing divisions.

Future plans

To achieve its goals, Banksbest and the digital transformation programme team are working on a number of different initiatives. These include the flagship 'My Way' project, which will allow business banking customers to access services however suits them best. Commissioned by the CDO and led by a product owner, My Way will allow business banking customers to use a range of devices to manage their accounts and move seamlessly between branch-based and online transactions. The current plans include:

- Testing biometrics including fingerprint and voice login to support My Way;
- My Deposit My Way, allowing cheques to be paid in using the camera on a mobile phone; and
- Monitoring of customer feedback, levels of demand and which products are most popular.

After three months, the product owner will report back to the CDO. At this point, the project will either be allocated additional funding, will pivot, or will be closed down. My Way is being measured on both governance and compliance and customer satisfaction outcomes.

IT services

All the IT services are run from the head office and the Manchester data centre. Since the digital transformation programme started, more services are Cloud hosted by external providers. The main IT services are:

Appendix: Banksbest case study

Bizbank – the banking system used in the branches and customer service centre. This system contains customer account information and history, including current and savings accounts. Bizbank is hosted in the Manchester data centre, but there are plans to move it to a Cloud hosting service to improve its resilience. Bizbank incidents sometimes take a long time to resolve because the original developers have left, and documentation is poor.

Mortbank – the mortgage system used in branches and the customer service centre. As well as tracking existing mortgages, Mortbank has a credit-checking facility that supports mortgage approvals. Mortbank was developed by MortSys, which provides ongoing support and maintenance. MortSys is a small organisation and doesn't always respond within its agreed target times.

Mibank – an online self-service portal being developed as part of the My Way project. Mibank allows customers to check their accounts, move money between accounts, pay bills and receive cheques. The functionality of Mibank will expand as the My Way project progresses.

Banksec – Banksec is an identity-checking utility that is used by Bizbank, Mortbank and Mibank. Banksec uses two-factor authentication, and biometric capabilities are in development.

IT department

The IT department includes 50 staff split into 4 departments, under the CIO:

- Strategic Planning and Business Relationship Management.
- Service Management.

Appendix: Banksbest case study

- Development.
- Operations (including Service Desk).

IT has a good reputation generally, but business staff see the IT department as responsible for day-to-day operations and fixing things. The IT department's development role is less well understood. There is also some friction between the digital transformation programme staff and IT staff.

IT service management

Service management does not have a high profile in Banksbest.

The CIO holds a position at board level, and likes to be seen as dynamic and responsive, rather than process driven and bureaucratic. However, some recent service outages have led to a level of interest in service management best practices, as well as assessment of other ways of working including DevOps, Agile and Lean.

There are some culture issues in the IT department, including an 'us and them' attitude that means developers and operations staff don't always work well together.

Sample employee biographies

Lucy Jones	Lucy joined Banksbest as a graduate trainee five years ago. As part of her training, she spent six months in each of the major departments: Central Operations, Branches and Customer Services. During her time in Central Operations, she spent two months in Finance, two months in HR and two months in IT, including working on the Service Desk.

Appendix: Banksbest case study

	Following completion of her graduate trainee programme, Lucy was offered a job in HR, and worked there for three years. She was then offered a newly created role of Product Owner and is responsible for the 'My Way' project. Lucy has a good understanding of the Banksbest business units and the IT services that support them.
Doug Range	Doug has worked for Banksbest for 20 years since it was HW Banking. He started work as counter staff in one of the branches and worked his way up to branch manager. Some years ago, his branch was chosen to be one of the pilot locations for the rollout of Bizbank, and for two years he acted as a super-user for this system, logging the queries he handled on the service desk system. He has recently been promoted to a head office role, including training the customer service centre staff. Doug is working with Lucy on the My Way project, helping to provide customer intelligence, and ensuring the customer service centre staff are kept up to date.

FURTHER READING

IT Governance Publishing (ITGP) is the world's leading publisher for governance and compliance. Our industry-leading pocket guides, books, training resources and toolkits are written by real-world practitioners and thought leaders. They are used globally by audiences of all levels, from students to C-suite executives.

Our high-quality publications cover all IT governance, risk and compliance frameworks and are available in a range of formats. This ensures our customers can access the information they need in the way they need it.

Other resources you may find useful include:

- *ITIL® Foundation Essentials ITIL 4 Edition – The ultimate revision guide, second edition* by Claire Agutter,
  www.itgovernancepublishing.co.uk/product/itil-foundation-essentials-itil-4-edition-the-ultimate-revision-guide-second-edition
- *ITIL® 4 Essentials – Your essential guide for the ITIL 4 Foundation exam and beyond, second edition* by Claire Agutter,
  www.itgovernancepublishing.co.uk/product/itil-4-essentials-your-essential-guide-for-the-itil-4-foundation-exam-and-beyond-second-edition
- *ITSM, ITIL® 4 & ISO 20000 Toolkit* published by ITGP,
  www.itgovernance.co.uk/shop/product/itsm-itil-4-iso-20000-toolkit

Further reading

For more information on ITGP and branded publishing services, and to view our full list of publications, visit *www.itgovernancepublishing.co.uk*.

To receive regular updates from ITGP, including information on new publications in your area(s) of interest, sign up for our newsletter at *www.itgovernancepublishing.co.uk/topic/newsletter*.

Branded publishing

Through our branded publishing service, you can customise ITGP publications with your company's branding.

Find out more at *www.itgovernancepublishing.co.uk/topic/branded-publishing-services*.

Related services

ITGP is part of GRC International Group, which offers a comprehensive range of complementary products and services to help organisations meet their objectives.

For a full range of resources on ITIL visit *www.itgovernance.co.uk/shop/category/itil*.

Training services

The IT Governance training programme is built on our extensive practical experience designing and implementing management systems based on ISO standards, best practice and regulations.

Our courses help attendees develop practical skills and comply with contractual and regulatory requirements. They also support career development via recognised qualifications.

Further reading

Learn more about our training courses and view the full course catalogue at *www.itgovernance.co.uk/training*.

Professional services and consultancy

We are a leading global consultancy of IT governance, risk management and compliance solutions. We advise businesses around the world on their most critical issues and present cost-saving and risk-reducing solutions based on international best practice and frameworks.

We offer a wide range of delivery methods to suit all budgets, timescales and preferred project approaches.

Find out how our consultancy services can help your organisation at *www.itgovernance.co.uk/consulting*.

Industry news

Want to stay up to date with the latest developments and resources in the IT governance and compliance market? Subscribe to our Weekly Round-up newsletter and we will send you mobile-friendly emails with fresh news and features about your preferred areas of interest, as well as unmissable offers and free resources to help you successfully start your projects. *www.itgovernance.co.uk/weekly-round-up*.

CPSIA information can be obtained
at www.ICGtesting.com
Printed in the USA
FSHW021702170321
79510FS